History 4
Student Guide

Part 2

About K12 Inc.

K12 Inc., a technology-based education company, is the nation's leading provider of proprietary curriculum and online education programs to students in grades K–12. K12 provides its curriculum and academic services to online schools, traditional classrooms, blended school programs, and directly to families. K12 Inc. also operates the K12 International Academy, an accredited, diploma-granting online private school serving students worldwide. K12's mission is to provide any child the curriculum and tools to maximize success in life, regardless of geographic, financial, or demographic circumstances. K12 Inc. is accredited by CITA. More information can be found at www.K12.com.

978-1-60153-317-3

Printed by Courier, Kendallville, IN, USA, April 2014, Lot 042014

Table of Contents

Student Worksheets and Assessments

Unit 10: World War II

Unit 11: Rebuilding a Better World

Student Guide
Lesson 1: Livingstone and Stanley in Africa

As the industrial nations of Europe grew stronger, they began to think about overseas empires. Soon they were carving the world into colonies. Even the United States won a few overseas territories in war. Nations competed to have the most colonies, the most industry, and the greatest military power. A new age of empire-building, or imperialism, had begun.

Scottish doctor David Livingstone went to Africa as a missionary. He explored the continent and was missing for several years. A reporter named Henry Stanley found him and later traveled with him. The adventures of both men excited European interest in Africa.

Lesson Objectives

- Describe "imperialism" as the push to create empires overseas.
- Recognize that the "age of imperialism" came at the end of the nineteenth and early twentieth centuries.
- Explain that industrial nations wanted colonies for more resources and naval bases.
- Describe Africa as nearly completely colonized by different European nations.
- Explain the phrase "the sun never sets on the British empire".
- Identify some famous figures and events in this period (David Livingstone, Henry Stanley, Ferdinand de Lesseps, Rudyard Kipling, Kaiser Wilhelm, Theodore Roosevelt; building of Suez Canal; the Spanish-American War).
- Locate on a map some of the major colonies of Great Britain, France, Germany, and territories owned by the United States.
- Define *imperialism* as the drive to create empires overseas.
- Explain that David Livingstone was a Scottish missionary and doctor who explored Africa, and that Henry Stanley was sent to find him.
- Recognize the phrase "Dr. Livingstone, I presume?" as the first words spoken by Stanley to Livingstone in Africa.
- Explain that reports about the adventures of Livingstone and Stanley excited European interest in Africa.

PREPARE

Approximate lesson time is 60 minutes.

Materials

For the Student

- Colonial Africa Color Map
- Africa in the Age of Imperialism
- map of Colonial Africa, circa 1900
- map of Colonial Africa, circa 1900 (color)

Keywords and Pronunciation

imperialism : The drive to build an empire or gain colonies overseas.

missionary : A person who spreads his or her religious faith to others.

Zambezi (zam-BEE-zee)

LEARN
Activity 1: The Scramble for Africa (Online)

Activity 2: History Journal (Offline)

It's time to add another chapter to the story of the past. Follow the directions to complete a new entry in your History Journal.

Turn to a new page in your History Journal. On this page, write a paragraph that tells what the lesson was about.

Begin with a topic sentence that introduces the paragraph. Include at least three sentences that give details about the lesson. End with a concluding sentence. You may use the Show You Know questions to help you get started.

When you have finished, check your work. Make sure you have written in complete sentences. Check to make sure you used correct capitalization and punctuation. Date your entry and label it with the lesson title.

Guided Learning: Compare your paragraph with the one in the Teacher Guide.

Activity 3: Africa in the Age of Imperialism (Offline)

Print the Africa in the Age of Imperialism activity sheet and the map of Colonial Africa, circa 1900. You'll also need to view the color version of this map. When you have completed the activity sheet, check your answers with those found in the Teacher Guide.

ASSESS
Lesson Assessment: Livingstone and Stanley in Africa (Online)

You will complete an online assessment covering the main objectives of this lesson. Your assessment will be scored by the computer.

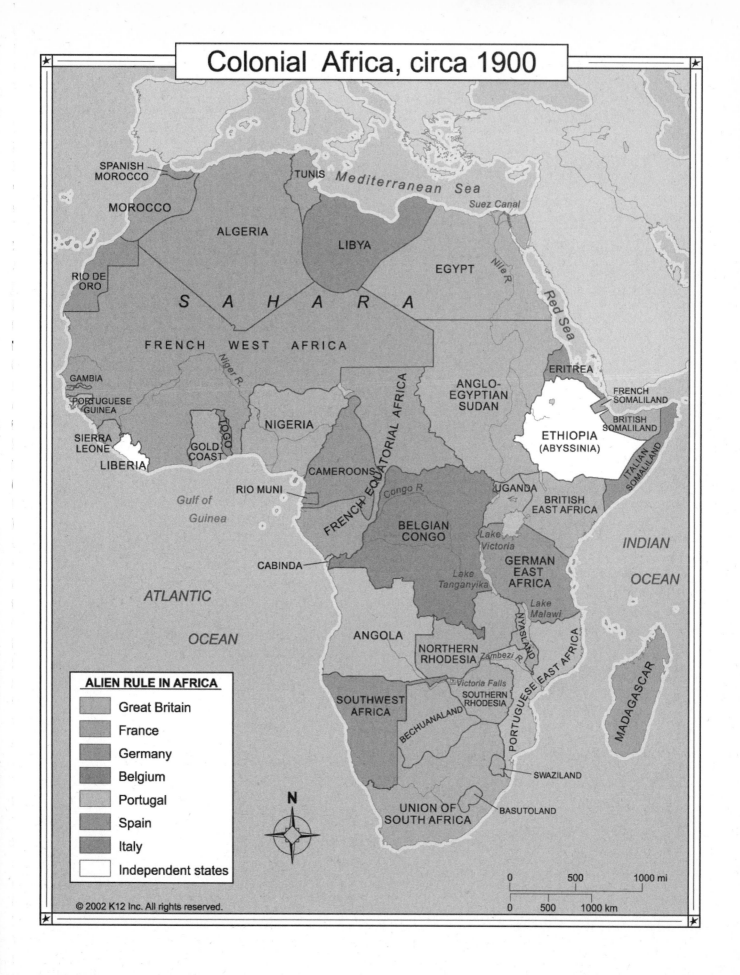

Colonial Africa, circa 1900

ALIEN RULE IN AFRICA

- Great Britain
- France
- Germany
- Belgium
- Portugal
- Spain
- Italy
- Independent states

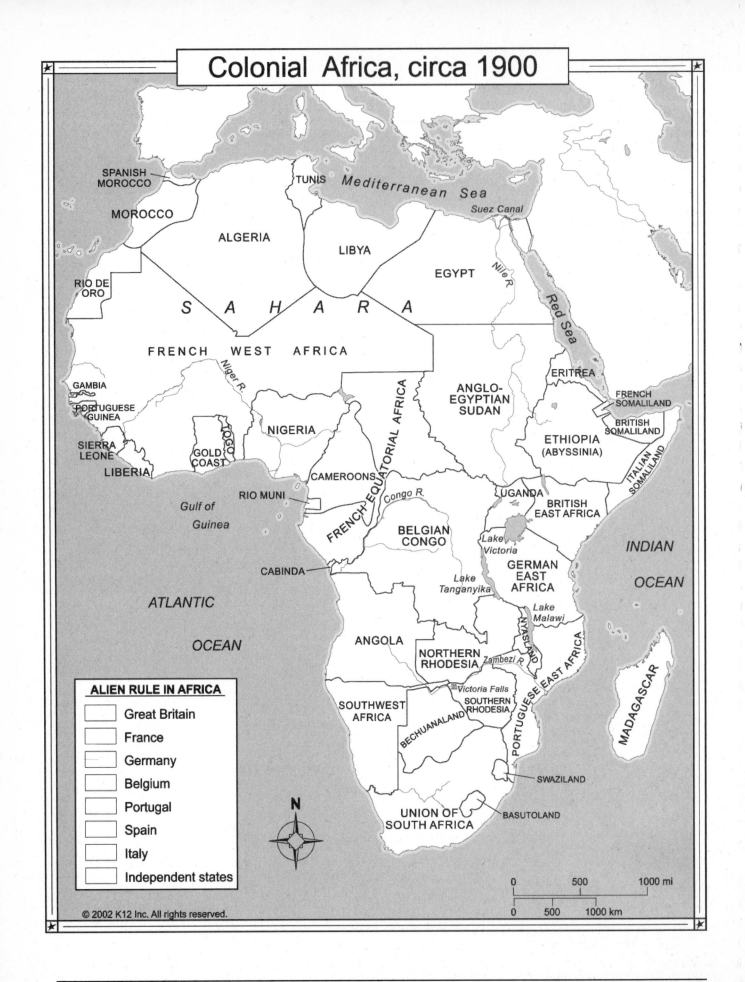

Colonial Africa, circa 1900

SPANISH MOROCCO

TUNIS

Mediterranean Sea

Suez Canal

MOROCCO

ALGERIA

LIBYA

EGYPT

RIO DE ORO

Nile R.

S   A   H   A   R   A

Red Sea

FRENCH   WEST   AFRICA

Niger R.

GAMBIA

PORTUGUESE GUINEA

ANGLO-EGYPTIAN SUDAN

ERITREA

FRENCH SOMALILAND

FRENCH EQUATORIAL AFRICA

NIGERIA

TOGO

SIERRA LEONE

GOLD COAST

BRITISH SOMALILAND

ETHIOPIA (ABYSSINIA)

ITALIAN SOMALILAND

LIBERIA

CAMEROONS

UGANDA

BRITISH EAST AFRICA

Congo R.

RIO MUNI

Gulf of Guinea

BELGIAN CONGO

Lake Victoria

ATLANTIC

CABINDA

GERMAN EAST AFRICA

INDIAN

Lake Tanganyika

OCEAN

Lake Malawi

OCEAN

NYASALAND

ANGOLA

NORTHERN RHODESIA

Zambezi R.

PORTUGUESE EAST AFRICA

MADAGASCAR

ALIEN RULE IN AFRICA

	Great Britain
	France
	Germany
	Belgium
	Portugal
	Spain
	Italy
	Independent states

Victoria Falls

SOUTHWEST AFRICA

SOUTHERN RHODESIA

BECHUANALAND

SWAZILAND

N

UNION OF SOUTH AFRICA

BASUTOLAND

0   500   1000 mi

0   500   1000 km

© 2002 K12 Inc. All rights reserved.

4

Name _____   Date _____

Africa in the Age of Imperialism

David Livingstone was a great Scottish explorer and Christian missionary in Africa. He spent years exploring the continent's interior.

1. What amazing natural feature did Livingstone see while he was exploring the Zambezi River?

    _____

On the map of Colonial Africa, circa 1900 (black and white), trace over the Zambezi River with a blue colored pencil.

Livingstone returned to England and became a national hero. He wrote a book and gave talks about his adventures in Africa. His reports fascinated Europeans. Soon European governments were scrambling to carve up Africa for themselves. They were seeking colonies to expand their empires.

2. What word refers to the drive to create empires overseas?

    _____

3. Into what body of water does the Nile River flow?

    _____

4. In what country is the mouth of the Nile located? _____

Trace over the Nile River with a blue colored pencil.

Livingstone did not find the source of the Nile River. Instead, he disappeared into the middle of the continent. Henry Stanley, a newspaper reporter, went to look for Livingstone.

Stanley found Livingstone near the shores of Lake Tanganyika. Color the lake blue on your map.

5. What did Stanley say to Livingstone when he found him?

_____

After Livingstone's death, European governments divided nearly all the continent among themselves.

6. What two countries claimed most of Africa?

_____

On the map, color the countries green that Great Britain claimed. Do you see any connection between the areas that Livingstone explored and the areas that Great Britain claimed?

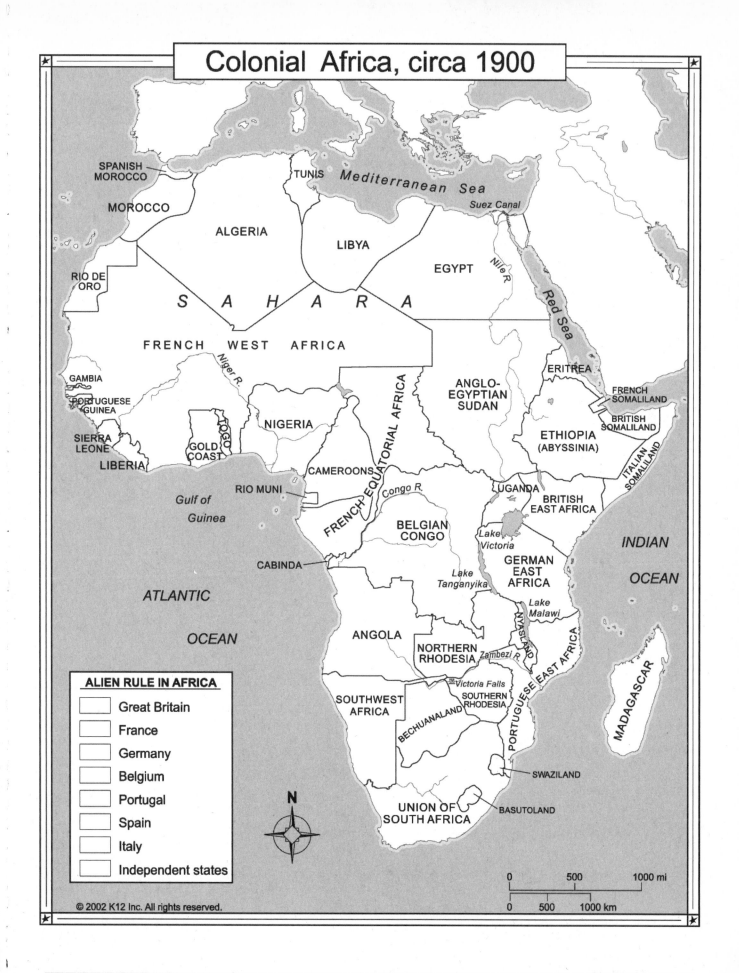

Colonial Africa, circa 1900

SPANISH MOROCCO
TUNIS
Mediterranean Sea
Suez Canal
MOROCCO
ALGERIA
LIBYA
EGYPT
Nile R.
RIO DE ORO
S A H A R A
Red Sea
FRENCH WEST AFRICA
GAMBIA
Niger R.
ANGLO-EGYPTIAN SUDAN
ERITREA
FRENCH SOMALILAND
PORTUGUESE GUINEA
NIGERIA
BRITISH SOMALILAND
SIERRA LEONE
GOLD COAST
TOGO
ETHIOPIA (ABYSSINIA)
LIBERIA
CAMEROONS
ITALIAN SOMALILAND
RIO MUNI
Gulf of Guinea
FRENCH EQUATORIAL AFRICA
Congo R.
UGANDA
BRITISH EAST AFRICA
BELGIAN CONGO
Lake Victoria
CABINDA
GERMAN EAST AFRICA
Lake Tanganyika
INDIAN OCEAN
ATLANTIC OCEAN
Lake Malawi
ANGOLA
NORTHERN RHODESIA
Zambezi R.
NYASALAND
PORTUGUESE EAST AFRICA
SOUTHWEST AFRICA
SOUTHERN RHODESIA
Victoria Falls
MADAGASCAR
BECHUANALAND
SWAZILAND
N
UNION OF SOUTH AFRICA
BASUTOLAND

ALIEN RULE IN AFRICA
- Great Britain
- France
- Germany
- Belgium
- Portugal
- Spain
- Italy
- Independent states

| 0 | 500 | 1000 mi |
| 0 | 500 | 1000 km |

Student Guide
Lesson 2: The French and the Suez Canal

The French built it in the 1800s. People from all over the world applauded when it was finished. Was it the Eiffel Tower? No. It was the Suez Canal in Egypt. It connected the Mediterranean and Red Seas.

Lesson Objectives

- Locate the Mediterranean Sea, Isthmus of Suez, Gulf of Suez, Red Sea, and Suez Canal on a map.
- Explain that the Suez Canal connected the Mediterranean Sea and Red Sea, making it possible to travel much more quickly between Europe and Asia.
- Explain that the French built the Suez Canal.
- Identify Ferdinand de Lesseps as the French engineer in charge of building the Suez Canal.

PREPARE

Approximate lesson time is 60 minutes.

Materials

For the Student

▣ Map of the Suez Canal, 1869

globe

History Journal

▣ Mapping the Suez Canal

Keywords and Pronunciation

canal : A man-made waterway.

cholera (KAH-luh-ruh)

Ferdinand de Lesseps (furd-ee-NAHN duh lay-SEPS)

isthmus (IS-muhs) : a narrow strip of land with water on both sides that connects two larger pieces of landPhonetic pronunciationIS-mus

Suez (SOO-ez)

LEARN
Activity 1: Digging a Ditch in the Desert *(Online)*

The French built it. The Ottoman Turks and Egyptians helped pay for it. The British would own it. Read on to learn the story of the Suez Canal.

Activity 2: History Journal (Offline)

It's time to add another chapter to the story of the past. Follow the directions to complete a new entry in your History Journal.

Turn to a new page in your History Journal. On this page, write a paragraph that tells what the lesson was about.

Begin with a topic sentence that introduces the paragraph. Include at least three sentences that give details about the lesson. End with a concluding sentence. You may use the Show You Know questions to help you get started.

When you have finished, check your work. Make sure you have written in complete sentences. Check to make sure you used correct capitalization and punctuation. Date your entry and label it with the lesson title.

Guided Learning: Compare your paragraph with the one in the Teacher Guide.

Activity 3: Mapping the Suez Canal (Offline)

Print and complete the Mapping the Suez Canal activity sheet. This activity sheet will be used as the assessment for today's lesson.

ASSESS

Lesson Assessment: The French and the Suez Canal (Online)

Have an adult review your answers to the Mapping the Suez Canal activity sheet and input the results online.

Name _____   Date _____

Mapping the Suez Canal

The building of the Suez Canal was an engineering marvel. It also had a great impact on world trade.

1. On the map below, label the following:

- Mediterranean Sea
- Isthmus of Suez
- Gulf of Suez

- Red Sea
- Suez Canal

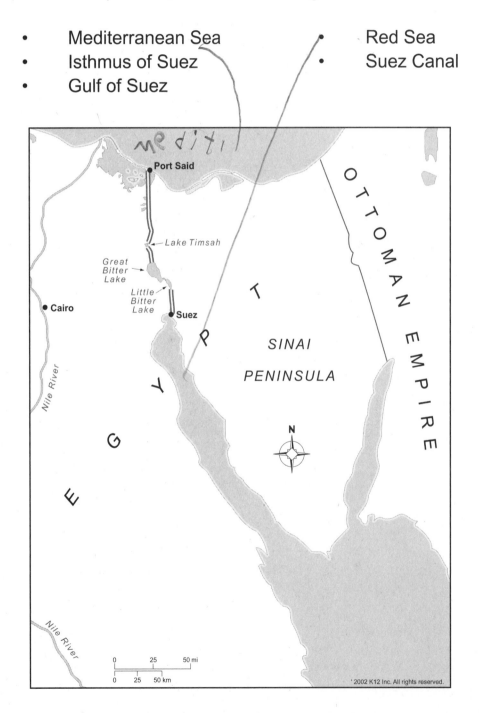

2. What two bodies of water does the Suez Canal connect?

    Mediterranean   Red Sea

3. Which country built the Suez Canal? France

4. Who was the engineer in charge of building the Suez Canal?

    Ferdinand de Lesseps

5. What was an important outcome of the building of the Suez Canal? (Hint: Think "trade.")

    Suez canal

6. Trace the shortest route a ship would have taken from England to China before the Suez Canal was built. In another color, trace the shortest route a ship could take from England to China after the canal was built.

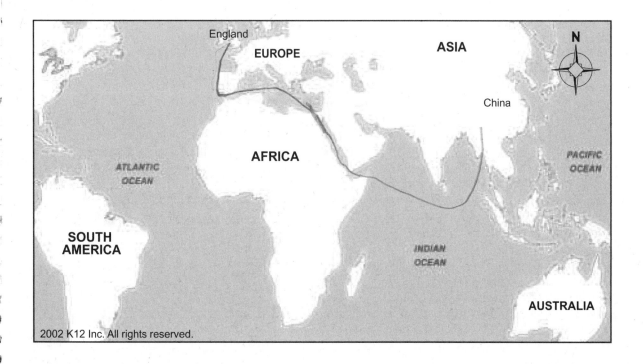

2002 K12 Inc. All rights reserved.

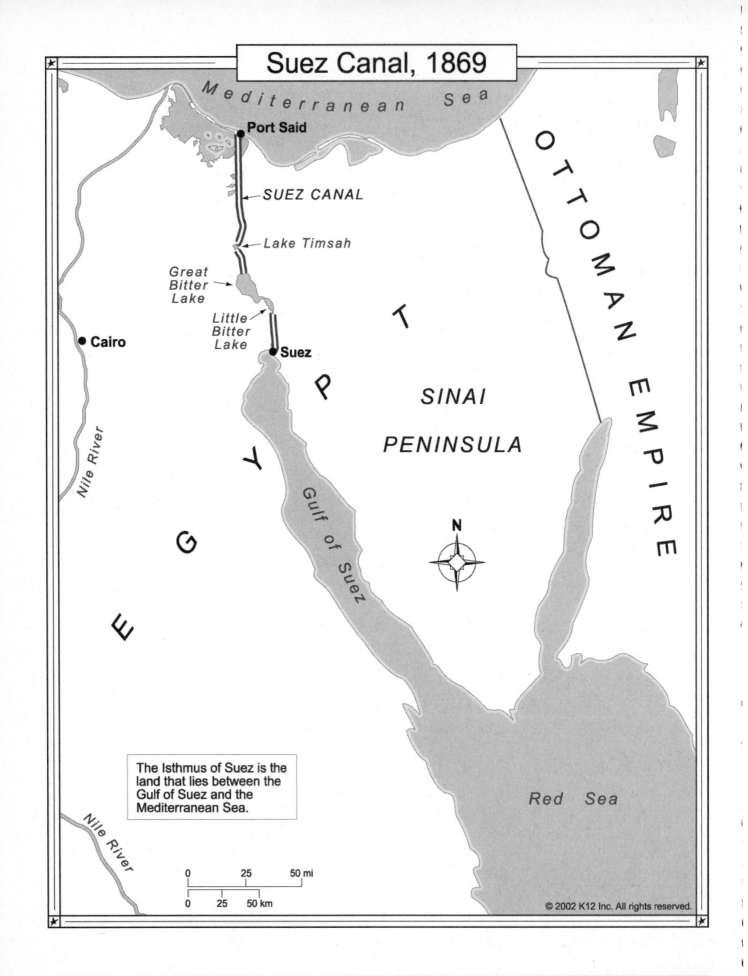

Suez Canal, 1869

Mediterranean Sea

Port Said

SUEZ CANAL

Lake Timsah

Great Bitter Lake

Little Bitter Lake

Suez

Cairo

Nile River

E G Y P T

SINAI PENINSULA

Gulf of Suez

OTTOMAN EMPIRE

N

Red Sea

The Isthmus of Suez is the land that lies between the Gulf of Suez and the Mediterranean Sea.

Nile River

| 0 | 25 | 50 mi |
| 0 | 25 | 50 km |

Name _____   Date _____

Mapping the Suez Canal

The building of the Suez Canal was an engineering marvel. It also had a great impact on world trade.

1. On the map below, label the following:

    - Mediterranean Sea
    - Isthmus of Suez
    - Gulf of Suez

    - Red Sea
    - Suez Canal

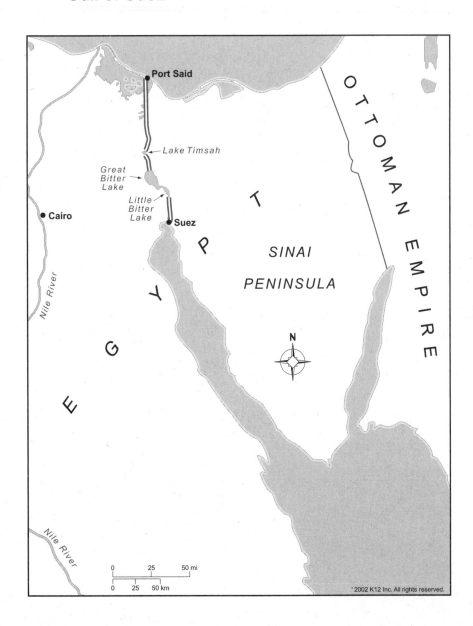

2. What two bodies of water does the Suez Canal connect?

    _____   _____

3. Which country built the Suez Canal? _____

4. Who was the engineer in charge of building the Suez Canal?

    _____

5. What was an important outcome of the building of the Suez
    Canal? (Hint: Think "trade.")

    _____

    _____

Student Guide
Lesson 3: Rudyard Kipling: Author and Advocate for Empire

Have you read *The Jungle Book* or the *Just So Stories*? Meet the author, Rudyard Kipling. This British writer grew up in India while it was a colony of Great Britain. He loved India, and he loved the British Empire.

Lesson Objectives

- Locate India on the globe and describe it as a British colony in the 1800s.
- Recognize Rudyard Kipling as a great British writer who wrote about India.
- Explain that Kipling wrote children's stories.
- Explain that Kipling celebrated the British Empire in his writings.

PREPARE

Approximate lesson time is 60 minutes.

Materials

> For the Student
>> globe

LEARN
Activity 1: India, the Jewel in the British Crown *(Online)*
Read about Rudyard Kipling, poet of the British Empire.

Activity 2: History Journal *(Offline)*
It's time to add another chapter to the story of the past. Follow the directions to complete a new entry in your History Journal.

Turn to a new page in your History Journal. On this page, write the answers to the following questions. Your work will be used to assess how well you understood the lesson.

1. How would you describe India in the 1800s? (Was it a colony or an independent nation? What nation was it closely connected with?)
2. Who was Rudyard Kipling?
3. What land was the subject of most of Kipling's work?
4. Who did Kipling write for, besides adults?
5. What did Kipling celebrate in his writings?

Activity 3: News of Kipling *(Offline)*

Print the Student Guide and follow the instructions.

Rudyard Kipling's first job in India was as a newspaper reporter. He wrote news articles, but he also began writing short stories.

Now you be the newspaper reporter. Imagine you're a reporter for a London newspaper. You've been sent to India to gather information for an article on Rudyard Kipling.

Remember that newspaper articles begin with something called a *lead.* The lead is a short paragraph. It answers most or all of the "five W's"--*who, what, why, when,* and *where.* One purpose of the lead is grab the reader's attention. Another is to help readers quickly learn the most important facts.

Here are some ways to write a lead:

- Write a sentence or two summing up the whole event.
- Start with a quotation from someone involved in the event.
- Describe the scene where the event took place.
- Ask an interesting question to catch the reader's attention

In the second paragraph, add more details. You can also try to answer the question of *how.* Write a brief, two-paragraph article about the great writer.

ASSESS

Lesson Assessment: Rudyard Kipling: Author and Advocate for Empire

(*Online*)

Have an adult review your answers to your History Journal entry and input the results online.

Lesson Assessment

Rudyard Kipling: Author and Advocate for Empire

Your student was asked the following questions in the Lesson's History Journal entry. Evaluate your student's responses in the activity and input the results online.

1. How would you describe India in the 1800s? (Was it a colony or an independent nation? What nation was it closely connected with?)

2. Who was Rudyard Kipling?

3. What land was the subject of most of Kipling's work?

4. Who did Kipling write for, besides adults?

5. What did Kipling celebrate in his writings?

Student Guide
Lesson 4: Germany's "Place in the Sun"

Kaiser Wilhelm II of Germany wanted his young nation to have its "place in the sun." He wanted a powerful country. Germany established colonies in Africa and Asia, and a strong German navy to protect them.

Lesson Objectives

- Explain that Germany was becoming a powerful industrial nation.
- Identify Kaiser Wilhelm II as the emperor of Germany.
- Explain that Kaiser Wilhelm II wanted Germany to be a great nation with overseas colonies and a strong navy.
- Explain that Great Britain, France, and other European nations grew fearful of German ambition.

PREPARE

Approximate lesson time is 60 minutes.

Materials

> For the Student
>
> > globe
> >
> > 🖵 map of Colonial Africa, circa 1900

Keywords and Pronunciation

Bremerhaven (BREH-mur-hah-vuhn)

kaiser (KIY-zur) : Emperor of Germany.

Wilhelm (VIL-helm)

LEARN
Activity 1: The Kaiser Takes Charge *(Online)*

Kaiser Wilhelm II of Germany was proud of the strong, new, unified Germany. He wanted to show the world just how great Germany was.

Activity 2: History Journal *(Offline)*

It's time to add another chapter to the story of the past. Follow the directions to complete a new entry in your History Journal.

Turn to a new page in your History Journal. On this page, write a paragraph that tells what the lesson was about.

Begin with a topic sentence that introduces the paragraph. Include at least three sentences that give details about the lesson. End with a concluding sentence. You may use the Show You Know questions to help you get started.

When you have finished, check your work. Make sure you have written in complete sentences. Check to make sure you used correct capitalization and punctuation. Date your entry and label it with the lesson title.

Guided Learning: Compare your paragraph with the one in the Teacher Guide.

Activity 3: Carving up Africa *(Offline)*

Print the Student Guide and the map of Colonial Africa, circa 1900 to get started. You'll need to view the color version of the map of <u>Colonial Africa,</u> to complete the activity. When you have finished, consult the Teacher Guide to check your answers.

By the late 1800s Germany had colonies along the west coast of Africa, in southwest Africa, and in east Africa too. Other European nations were expanding their overseas empires as well, carving out colonies from the African continent.

For the following activity, shade areas on the map of Colonial Africa, circa 1900 lightly with colored pencils. Use the online color version of the map as a reference.

· Color all of Germany's colonies brown.

· Color Great Britain's colonies green.

· Color France's colonies purple.

Answer the following questions in your History Journal. (You can write the answers below today's journal entry.)

1. Which two countries had claimed most of Africa by 1900?
2. What were the only two independent nations in Africa at this time?
3. Which three colonies were part of Portugal's empire?
4. Which other nations had only three colonies in Africa?
5. What was Belgium's only colony in Africa?
6. Whose colony did the Suez Canal run through?
7. What country controlled both sides of the Straits of Gibraltar?

ASSESS

Lesson Assessment: Germany's "Place in the Sun" (*Online*)

You will complete an online assessment covering the main objectives of this lesson. Your assessment will be scored by the computer.

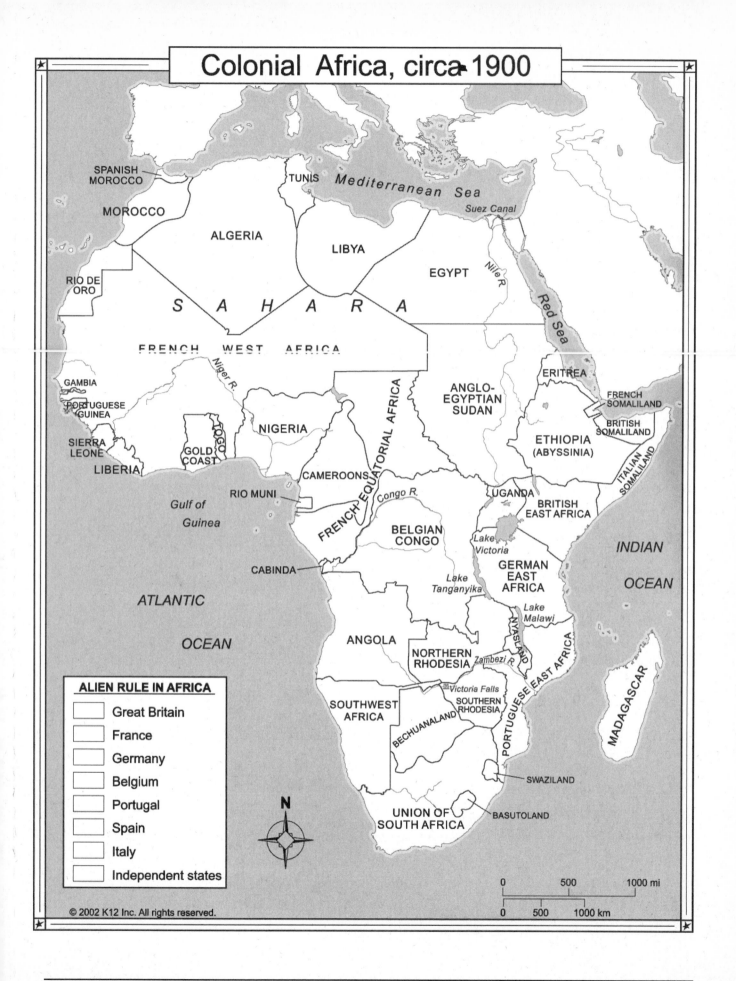

Colonial Africa, circa 1900

SPANISH MOROCCO

MOROCCO

TUNIS

Mediterranean Sea

Suez Canal

RIO DE ORO

ALGERIA

LIBYA

EGYPT

Nile R.

Red Sea

S A H A R A

FRENCH WEST AFRICA

Niger R.

GAMBIA

PORTUGUESE GUINEA

SIERRA LEONE

LIBERIA

GOLD COAST

TOGO

NIGERIA

CAMEROONS

RIO MUNI

Gulf of Guinea

FRENCH EQUATORIAL AFRICA

Congo R.

ANGLO-EGYPTIAN SUDAN

ERITREA

FRENCH SOMALILAND

BRITISH SOMALILAND

ETHIOPIA (ABYSSINIA)

ITALIAN SOMALILAND

UGANDA

BRITISH EAST AFRICA

BELGIAN CONGO

Lake Victoria

CABINDA

Lake Tanganyika

GERMAN EAST AFRICA

Lake Malawi

ATLANTIC

OCEAN

ANGOLA

NORTHERN RHODESIA

Zambezi R.

NYASALAND

PORTUGUESE EAST AFRICA

INDIAN

OCEAN

Victoria Falls

SOUTHERN RHODESIA

SOUTHWEST AFRICA

BECHUANALAND

MADAGASCAR

SWAZILAND

N

UNION OF SOUTH AFRICA

BASUTOLAND

ALIEN RULE IN AFRICA

- Great Britain
- France
- Germany
- Belgium
- Portugal
- Spain
- Italy
- Independent states

| 0 | 500 | 1000 mi |
| 0 | 500 | 1000 km |

© 2002 K12 Inc. All rights reserved.

Student Guide
Lesson 5: "A Splendid Little War": The Spanish-American War

Europeans weren't the only ones who expanded their reach in the Age of Imperialism. The United States fought a war to help Cuba gain independence from Spain. The United States ended up with a few overseas territories of its own.

Lesson Objectives

- Describe the Spanish-American War as a war in which the United States gained overseas territories.
- Identify territories gained by the United States during the Spanish-American War (the Philippines, Guam, Puerto Rico).
- Identify Theodore Roosevelt as an American leader who helped free Cuba and was a strong advocate for America's military strength.

PREPARE

Approximate lesson time is 60 minutes.

Materials

For the Student

globe

Teddy Roosevelt: Young Rough Rider by Edd Winfield Parks

Keywords and Pronunciation

Guam (gwahm)

Philippines (FIH-luh-peenz)

Puerto Rico (PWEHR-toh REE-koh)

San Juan (san wahn)

Santiago (san-tee-AH-goh)

LEARN
Activity 1: America Rebuilds *(Online)*

Grab your globe and get ready to take it for a spin. It was the Age of Imperialism and the United States found itself in control of territories near and far.

Activity 2: History Journal *(Offline)*

It's time to add another chapter to the story of the past. Follow the directions to complete a new entry in your History Journal.

Turn to a new page in your History Journal. On this page, write a paragraph that tells what the lesson was about.

Begin with a topic sentence that introduces the paragraph. Include at least three sentences that give details about the lesson. End with a concluding sentence. You may use the Show You Know questions to help you get started.

When you have finished, check your work. Make sure you have written in complete sentences. Check to make sure you used correct capitalization and punctuation. Date your entry and label it with the lesson title.

Guided Learning: Compare your paragraph with the one in the Teacher Guide.

Activity 3: The Questions Is, "Who Was T.R.?" (Offline)

Demonstrate your knowledge of Theodore Roosevelt by writing some quiz show material.

Imagine you're one of the writers for a quiz show. Next week's show is about American presidents. You've been assigned Theodore Roosevelt. (Roosevelt was often called "T.R.")

In your History Journal, write a list of answers to the question "Who was Theodore Roosevelt?" For example:

Question: Who was Theodore Roosevelt?

Answer: A U.S. president who was a sickly boy, but grew up to be a good athlete.

If you're having trouble thinking what to write, reread *Roosevelt's Rough Riders*.

Guided Learning: When you've finished, check your work against the examples in the Teacher Guide.

ASSESS

Lesson Assessment: "A Splendid Little War": The Spanish-American War (*Online*)

You will complete an online assessment covering the main objectives of this lesson. Your assessment will be scored by the computer.

LEARN

Activity 4. Optional: "A Splendid Little War": The Spanish-American War (Offline)

For a biography of Theodore Roosevelt, check your library or local bookstore for *Teddy Roosevelt: Young Rough Rider* by Edd Winfield Parks, illustrated by Gray Morrow (New York: Aladdin Paperbacks, 1989).

Student Guide
Lesson 6: Unit Review and Assessment

You've completed this unit, and now it's time to review what you've learned and take the unit assessment.

Lesson Objectives

- Demonstrate mastery of important knowledge and skills taught in previous lessons.
- Demonstrate mastery of important knowledge and skills in this unit.
- Explain that David Livingstone was a Scottish missionary and doctor who explored Africa, and that Henry Stanley was sent to find him.
- Explain that reports about the adventures of Livingstone and Stanley excited European interest in Africa.
- Locate the Mediterranean Sea, Isthmus of Suez, Gulf of Suez, Red Sea, and Suez Canal on a map.
- Explain that the Suez Canal connected the Mediterranean Sea and Red Sea, making it possible to travel much more quickly between Europe and Asia.
- Explain that the French built the Suez Canal.
- Identify Ferdinand de Lesseps as the French engineer in charge of building the Suez Canal.
- Locate India on the globe and describe it as a British colony in the 1800s.
- Recognize Rudyard Kipling as a great British writer who wrote about India.
- Explain that Germany was becoming a powerful industrial nation.
- Identify Kaiser Wilhelm II as the emperor of Germany.
- Explain that Kaiser Wilhelm II wanted Germany to be a great nation with overseas colonies and a strong navy.
- Explain that Great Britain, France, and other European nations grew fearful of German ambition.
- Recognize that the "age of imperialism" came at the end of the nineteenth and early twentieth centuries.
- Explain that industrial nations wanted colonies for more resources and naval bases.
- Describe Africa as nearly completely colonized by different European nations.
- Explain the phrase "the sun never sets on the British empire".
- Locate on a map some of the major colonies of Great Britain, France, Germany, and territories owned by the United States.

PREPARE

Approximate lesson time is 60 minutes.

LEARN
Activity 1: The Age of Imperialism (Offline)

We've covered a lot, and now it's time to take a look back. Here's what you should remember about the Age of Imperialism.

We've been learning about the "Age of Imperialism," which came at the end of the nineteenth century and the beginning of the twentieth century.

Nations were thinking about empires overseas. You've learned that feelings of nationalism had grown strong in Europe and America. New industries were booming. Colonies overseas could provide more resources to run those booming industries--resources such as coal and iron. Colonies overseas also meant new ports for growing navies.

Should the industrial nations have colonies in Africa? in China? in India? in the Pacific? The Africans, Chinese, and Indians didn't think so. But nobody asked them. The new industrial nations just came.

Heading first to Africa was a famous British doctor and missionary. He didn't go there to start colonies. He went to help the sick and spread the Christian faith. He explored as he went. He saw the beauty of a waterfall he named "Victoria Falls," and he sailed down the Zambezi River. What was the name of that famous doctor? [1]

Livingstone wrote about his journeys and went back to England to speak about them. He awakened a lively interest in Africa. Then he went back to Africa to explore some more. Europeans and Americans thought he had gotten lost. A New York newspaper sent a reporter to Africa to find him. Who was that reporter? [2]

Stanley and Livingstone journeyed together for a while. Soon the British began establishing colonies in Africa. The British weren't the only Europeans interested in Africa. Which other European nation had colonies in North Africa? [3]

A French engineer in North Africa, named Ferdinand de Lesseps, had an idea for a way to make travel between Europe and its colonies easier. What did Ferdinand de Lesseps want to build? [4]

The Egyptians liked the idea and said they would help out. The Suez Canal connected the Mediterranean and the Red Seas.

On a globe or world map, point to the location of the Suez Canal. (Hint: It's the place where the Mediterranean Sea and Red Sea nearly touch each other.)

The Canal made it a lot faster and easier to travel between Europe and what other continent? [5]

Although they didn't build the canal, which European nation benefited the most from it? [6]

The British benefited most from the Suez Canal because they had an important colony in Asia. Now they could get there faster. They said that Asian colony was "the jewel in the British crown." Which colony was that? [7]

A famous British writer grew up in India and wrote children's stories about the animals and jungles of India. Who was that author? [8]

Rudyard Kipling also wrote poems celebrating the huge British Empire. People said "the sun never sets on the British Empire." Why did they say that? [9]

While the British, the French, and other European nations were colonizing Africa and Asia, the German Kaiser got interested, too. What was the name of the German Kaiser who wanted Germany to be an imperial nation? [10]

What part of the German military did the Kaiser want to build up? (Hint: He wanted his to be as mighty as Great Britain's.) [11]

Soon the Germans had colonies in Africa and China. Now Africa was almost completely colonized by Europeans. And the Kaiser kept rattling his saber.

Far away from these European nations, the United States was recovering fast from its Civil War. Its industry was strong. Theodore Roosevelt wanted to make sure the U.S. Navy was strong too. He and most Americans wanted to get the Spanish out of "the American hemisphere." So in 1898 the United States went to war to free Cuba. What was that war called? [12]

What was the name of the group Theodore Roosevelt led up San Juan Hill? [13]

What did the United States gain as a result of the war? [14]

Because of its victory in the war, the United States suddenly had the Philippines, Guam, and Puerto Rico as overseas territories. For a short time Cuba was an American territory too.

Was it odd for the United States of America, a former British colony, to have colonies overseas? You bet! It was so odd, many Americans couldn't even bring themselves to call the territories "colonies." They called them "American territories." The idea was that the United States would protect these lands until they were ready to govern themselves. Then they would be free. Cuba became a free nation in a short time. The Philippines, Guam, and Puerto Rico remained American territories for a long time.

We've been learning about booming industrial nations stretching out during this Age of Imperialism. They wanted lots of colonies overseas. They were confident. They were just plain arrogant, too. They were sure that Africa, India, and China were better off under their control. They thought the people in those countries were backward and not as good as they were. We'll see, though, that human beings just love freedom and that great leaders would emerge from those colonies. The people of those colonies would challenge silly imperial ideas.

Meanwhile, the confidence of the industrial nations was having a good effect, too. That confidence helped inventors in the industrial nations develop new inventions and solve one scientific problem after another. We'll learn about all that in the next unit.

Activity 2: Online Interactive Review (Online)

ASSESS

Unit Assessment: The Age of Imperialism (Offline)

Complete an offline Unit Assessment. Your learning coach will score this part of the Assessment.

Name _____   Date _____

The Age of Imperialism

Read each question and its answer choices. Fill in the bubble in front of the best answer.

1. What is *imperialism*?

    ⓐ   the drive to create a capitalist economy

    ⓑ   the push to create empires overseas

    ⓒ   the hope of creating a united country

    ⓓ   the ability to make and sell goods

2. A desire for _____ prompted industrial nations to seek overseas colonies.

    ⓐ   spices and gold

    ⓑ   democratic revolutions

    ⓒ   more resources and naval bases

    ⓓ   scientific understanding of nature

3. What continent was almost completely colonized by European nations in the late nineteenth century?

    ⓐ   North America

    ⓑ   South America

    ⓒ   Africa

    ⓓ   Asia

4. "I was a British doctor and missionary who traveled to Africa to explore, help the sick, and spread the Christian faith. Who am I?"

   (a)   Ferdinand de Lesseps

   (b)   David Livingstone

   (c)   Rudyard Kipling

   (d)   Henry Stanley

5. What happened shortly after reports of the African adventures of Livingstone and Stanley were printed in newspapers?

   (a)   The Americans built the Suez Canal.

   (b)   Germany decided against building a navy.

   (c)   France made India a French colony.

   (d)   The British began to colonize parts of Africa.

6. Who built the Suez Canal?

   (a)   the British, led by David Stanley

   (b)   the Americans, led by Theodore Roosevelt

   (c)   the French, led by Ferdinand de Lesseps

   (d)   the Egyptians, led by Pasha Said

7. What two bodies of water did the Suez Canal connect?

   (a)   the Red Sea and the Persian Gulf

   (b)   the Mediterranean Sea and the Red Sea

   (c)   the Atlantic Ocean and the Pacific Ocean

   (d)   the Atlantic Ocean and the Mediterranean Sea

8. Why was the Suez Canal built?

   (a)   to reduce travel time between Europe and Asia

   (b)   to allow trading caravans easy access to Egypt

   (c)   to improve international relations between France and Egypt

   (d)   to make it easier to travel from Africa to South America

9. Which country benefited most from the construction of the Suez Canal?

   (a)   United States

   (b)   France

   (c)   Germany

   (d)   Great Britain

10. How would India in the 1800s be described?

   (a)   a free and independent nation

   (b)   a colony of Germany

   (c)   a colony of Great Britain

   (d)   an uninhabited and unexplored land

11. Who was Rudyard Kipling?

   (a)   an American explorer who traveled in Africa

   (b)   a British writer who wrote about Africa

   (c)   a British writer who wrote about India

   (d)   a German leader who colonized India

12. Why was it said that the "sun never sets on the British Empire"?

  ⓐ   All of Britain's colonies were in the east, where the sun rises.

  ⓑ   The British Empire was so large that it was always daytime somewhere.

  ⓒ   Japan, the "land of the rising sun," was a British colony.

  ⓓ   Great Britain invented and used daylight savings time in its empire.

13. Why was the Suez Canal so important to Great Britain?

  ⓐ   It employed thousands of British subjects.

  ⓑ   It shortened the travel time to India.

  ⓒ   It brought a lot of national pride to the nation.

  ⓓ   It caused Germany to stop its naval buildup.

14. In the late nineteenth century, Germany was becoming a _____ nation.

  ⓐ   weak and backward

  ⓑ   powerful industrial

  ⓒ   wealthy and divided

  ⓓ   poorly educated

15. Who reigned as emperor in Germany in the late nineteenth century?

  ⓐ   Otto von Bismarck

  ⓑ   Kaiser Wilhelm II

  ⓒ   Czar Nicholas II

  ⓓ   Theodore Roosevelt

16. What did this emperor want Germany to do?

   ⓐ   overthrow the Russian czars and rule Russia

   ⓑ   separate into smaller, weaker regions

   ⓒ   establish overseas colonies and a strong navy

   ⓓ   invade Egypt and build an important canal

17. At this time, what effect did changes in Germany have on other European countries, like Great Britain and France?

   ⓐ   They welcomed Germany's desire for greatness.

   ⓑ   They began to make plans to invade Germany.

   ⓒ   They reluctantly gave their colonies to Germany.

   ⓓ   They grew fearful of Germany's ambitious behavior.

18. When was the "age of imperialism"?

   ⓐ   the late 1600s and early 1700s

   ⓑ   the middle of the 1700s

   ⓒ   the late 1800s and early 1900s

   ⓓ   the middle and late 1900s

19. On the map below, label the following:

   1 - Suez Canal

   2 - British colony of India

   3 - French colony of Algeria

   4 - German colonies of German East Africa and Southwest Africa

20. Write a short paragraph about the Spanish-American War. In your paragraph:

  · Describe one outcome, or result, of the Spanish-American War.

  · Identify at least two overseas territories gained by the United States.

  · Name the American leader who helped free Cuba and tell how he felt about America's military.

Begin your paragraph with a topic sentence. Write neatly in complete sentences. Check your spelling, capitalization, and punctuation. End your paragraph with a concluding sentence.

_____

_____

_____

_____

_____

_____

_____

_____

_____

_____

_____

_____

_____

Student Guide
Lesson 1: Louis Pasteur

Invention fever! People caught it in Europe and America as the 1800s ended and the 1900s began. Inventions sped up communication and transportation. Inventors figured out new ways to cure diseases and link the seas. It was an age of confidence--a "can do" age.

The makers of wine and milk loved him. Who was he?
The great French scientist, Louis Pasteur. He figured out that bacteria caused problems for French wine and milk producers. Later, he discovered that bacteria sometimes spread human diseases.

Lesson Objectives

- Describe the late nineteenth and early twentieth centuries as an age of invention and enterprise.
- Explain that many great strides in medicine, industry, communication and transportation took place at this time.
- Identify some of the key innovators of the period (Pasteur, Samuel B. Morse, Thomas Edison, Alexander Graham Bell, Andrew Carnegie, Gustave Eiffel, Daimler and Benz, Henry Ford, Guglielmo Marconi, Orville and Wilbur Wright).
- Identify some of the major inventions, and innovations of the period (pasteurization, development of the telegraph, electric light, the telephone, steel industry, automobile, automobile factory, radio, airplanes, the Panama Canal).
- Describe Louis Pasteur as a great French scientist.
- Explain that Pasteur studied bacteria, and learned that it could sour food and spread disease.
- Explain that pasteurization is a process used on milk and other foods.
- Describe pasteurization as a process of using heat to kill bacteria.

PREPARE

Approximate lesson time is 60 minutes.

Materials

> For the Student
>> History Journal

Keywords and Pronunciation

Anton van Leeuwenhoek (AHN-tohn vahn LAY-ven-hook)

bacteria : a kind of microscopic organism.

germs : The common name for disease-causing bacteria.

Louis Pasteur (LOO-ee pas-TUR)

merci (MEHR-see)

Monsieur (muhs-yur)

pasteurization (pas-chuh-ruh-ZAY-shuhn) : A process of heating food to kill the germs that spoil it.

vintner : A wine maker.

LEARN
Activity 1: Pasteur Heats Things Up *(Online)*

Activity 2: History Journal *(Offline)*

It's time to add another chapter to the story of the past. Follow the directions to complete a new entry in your History Journal.

Turn to a new page in your History Journal and write a paragraph that summarizes the lesson.
Begin with a topic sentence that introduces the paragraph. Include at least three sentences that give details about the lesson. End with a concluding sentence. You may use the Show You Know questions to help you get started.
When you have finished, check your work. Make sure you have written complete sentences. Check to make sure you capitalized and punctuated everything correctly. Date your entry and label it with the lesson title.
Guided Learning: Compare your paragraph with the one in the Teacher Guide.

Activity 3: In Honor of Pasteur *(Offline)*

Write a short speech honoring Louis Pasteur. Your work will be used as the assessment for this lesson.

The year is 1880 and an aging Louis Pasteur is about to be awarded a special medal for his lifetime of accomplishments. Imagine you are one of his colleagues. You've been asked to give a short speech and present the award.
Write the one paragraph speech you will give. Describe his accomplishments and the impact they have on us today.
Answers to the following questions should be included in the speech:
1. Who was Louis Pasteur?
2. What did he study and what did he learn?
3. What is pasteurization?
4. What kinds of food is pasteurization used for?
Place your completed work in your History Journal.

Activity 4. Optional: Louis Pasteur *(Offline)*

Louis Pasteur said some interesting things. Pick one of his quotations and tell what you think he meant.

The following are four quotations from Louis Pasteur. Select one, write it in your History Journal, and then tell what you think he meant by it.
"The best proof that an observer has struck the right path is the constant fruitfulness of his work."
"In the realm of scientific observation, luck is granted only to those who are prepared."
"Science belongs to no one nation."

ASSESS

Lesson Assessment: Louis Pasteur (*Online*)

Have an adult review your History Journal essay and input the results in the assessment at the end of the lesson.

Lesson Assessment

Louis Pasteur

The year is 1880 and an aging Louis Pasteur is about to be awarded a special medal for his lifetime of accomplishments. Imagine you are one of his colleagues. You've been asked to give a short speech and present the award.

Write the one paragraph speech you will give. Describe his accomplishments and the impact they have on us today.

Answers to the following questions should be included in the speech:

1. Who was Louis Pasteur?
2. What did he study and what did he learn?
3. What is pasteurization?
4. What kinds of food is pasteurization used for?

Student Guide
Lesson 2: Speeding It Up: Telegraphs, Sewing Machines, and Typewriters

The Age of Invention produced machines that could speed up all sorts of things. The telegraph sped news across the country by wire. The typewriter made writing faster. And the sewing machine made it possible to make clothes a lot more quickly.

Lesson Objectives

- Explain that the telegraph was a means of rapid communication that used electric pulses to send messages by wire.
- Identify Samuel F. B. Morse as the inventor of the telegraph and the Morse code.
- Describe the Morse code as a series of clicks and pauses used to transmit messages.
- Describe the typewriter as the first practical writing machine.

PREPARE

Approximate lesson time is 60 minutes.

Materials

For the Student

Inventors: A Library of Congress Book by Martin Sandler

History Journal

📇 Dot Dash Dot Activity Sheet

Keywords and Pronunciation

patent : The right to make, use, or sell an invention.

LEARN
Activity 1: Communication Speeds Up (Offline)
Instructions
Print the Student Guide and follow the instructions.

Get Ready
In the "can-do" age, scientists and inventors set about solving problems that had stumped people for a long time. In France, Louis Pasteur helped wine makers solve the problem of wine that spoiled.

1. Why did wine spoil?
2. What solution did Pasteur find?
3. What other product is pasteruized today?
4. Pasteur discovered that germs could cause disease in humans. What remedy did he use to help stop the spread of rabies and other diseases?

Guided Learning: Check with an adult for the answers to these questions.

While Pasteur was making chemical breakthroughs, others were solving problems in communication, transportation, and manufacturing. Let's find out about the work of Samuel F. B. Morse and others.

The late 1800s produced a revolution in communication. Faster, better, faster, better, faster, faster, faster.... Everyone wanted information as fast as they could get it. After all, news wasn't "new" if it took weeks to reach people.

Nobody was more interested in speedy communication than Americans. They were settling a very large continent. How could people in California learn what was happening in New York? How could people in Texas learn about the market for beef in Chicago? Americans began to think hard about these problems. A great age of invention followed.

Read pages 7 - 13 (Forward and "An Inventive Spirit") in Inventors by Martin Sandler.

1. What was the mood of Americans in 1876?
2. Americans had been proud of political heroes such as George Washington and Thomas Jefferson. What new type of hero emerged in the late 1800s?
3. Look at the pictures on pages 12 and 13. What improvements in transportation developed during this time?

Guided Learning: Check with an adult for the answers to these questions.

Read pages 14-19 ("Products of Invention") in Inventors by Martin Sandler.

1. What was the telegraph?
2. Who was the inventor of the telegraph?
3. What was Morse code?
4. Why did some newspapers call themselves "The Daily Telegraph" or "The Telegrapher"?
5. How many miles of telegraph wire existed in the U.S. by 1883?
6. What machine helped women make clothes in their homes?
7. Who received a patent for a sewing machine and sold it in nations throughout the world?
8. What was the first practical writing machine?
9. What problem did Christopher Scholes have to solve to invent a workable typewriter?
10. Who used typewriters?

Guided Learning: Check with an adult for the answers to these questions.

The telegraph, the typewriter, and the sewing machine were just a few of the many inventions of the late 1800s. Communication improved and businesses operated more efficiently. But things would get even more interesting in the years to come--particularly in the laboratory of a real genius, Thomas Edison.

Show You Know

NOTE: Show You Know questions may not be necessary since we've asked so many questions in the lesson, but here are some in case you want to include them.

1. What was the telegraph?
2. Who invented the telegraph?
3. What was Morse Code?
4. What was the first practical writing machine?

Guided Learning: Check with an adult for the answers to these questions.

Activity 2: History Journal (Offline)

It's time to add another chapter to the story of the past. Follow the directions to complete a new entry in your History Journal.

Turn to a new page in your History Journal. On this page, write a paragraph that tells what the lesson was about.

Begin with a topic sentence that introduces the paragraph. Include at least three sentences that give details about the lesson. End with a concluding sentence. You may use the Show You Know questions to help you get started.

When you have finished, check your work. Make sure you have written complete sentences. Check to make sure you used correct capitalization and punctuation. Date your entry and label it with the lesson title.

Guided Learning: Compare your paragraph with the one in the Teacher Guide.

Activity 3: Dot Dash Dot (Offline)

Print the Dot Dash Dot activity sheet. Use it to learn a little Morse code. Try composing a message using Morse code.

ASSESS

Lesson Assessment: Speeding It Up: Telegraphs, Sewing Machines, and Typewriters (Offline)

You will complete an offline assessment covering the main objectives of this lesson. Your learning coach will score this assessment.

LEARN

Activity 4. Optional: Speeding It Up: Telegraphs, Sewing Machines, and Typewriters (Online)

Name _____ Date _____

Dot Dash Dot

In Morse code, each letter or number is represented by a dot or dash, or a series of dots and dashes.

The Alphabet

A	.−	G	−−.	M	−−	S	...	Y	−.−−
B	−...	H	....	N	−.	T	−	Z	−−..
C	−.−.	I	..	O	−−−	U	..−		
D	−..	J	.−−−	P	.−−.	V	...−		
E	.	K	−.−	Q	−−.−	W	.−−		
F	..−.	L	.−..	R	.−.	X	−..−		

Numbers

1	.−−−−	3	...−−	5	.....	7	−−...	9	−−−−.
2	..−−−	4	....−	6	−....	8	−−−..	0	−−−−−

Try deciphering this Morse code:

... .− −− ..− . .−.. ..−. −... −− −−− .−. ... .

Samuel F B Morse

Now translate the answer to this question into Morse code:

What was the first practical writing machine?

_____

The dots and dashes above are what you see when working with Morse code. But what do you hear? When amateur radio operators use Morse code to communicate with each other, they hear the Morse code.

A single dot sounds like this: dit.
A dash sounds like this: dah.
A dot that is followed by a dash sounds like this: di dah.

This is what the following letters would sound like:

A: di dah
M: dah dah
S: di di dit
Y: dah di dah dah

Translate the following:

dah di dah dah   dah dah dah   di di dah   di dah   di dah dit

dit   dah di dit   dah dah dah   dah dit   dit

_____

Student Guide
Lesson 3: The Wizard of Menlo Park: Thomas Edison

Thomas Edison was one of the greatest inventors of all time. He invented the first practical electric lightbulb. He invented the phonograph. He even invented a new way to invent. He called it the "Invention Factory."

Lesson Objectives

- Describe Edison as one of the greatest inventors of all time.
- Name the electric lightbulb as one of his inventions.
- Explain that Edison's "Invention Factory" became a model for industrial research laboratories.

PREPARE

Approximate lesson time is 60 minutes.

Materials

> For the Student
>> History Journal

Keywords and Pronunciation

phonograph : A device for playing music.

LEARN
Activity 1: Meet Thomas Edison *(Online)*

Activity 2: History Journal *(Offline)*

It's time to add another chapter to the story of the past. Follow the directions to complete a new entry in your History Journal.

Turn to a new page in your History Journal. On this page, write a paragraph that tells what the lesson was about.

Begin with a topic sentence that introduces the paragraph. Include at least three sentences that give details about the lesson. End with a concluding sentence. You may use the Show You Know questions to help you get started.

When you have finished, check your work. Make sure you have written in complete sentences. Check to make sure you used correct capitalization and punctuation. Date your entry and label it with the lesson title.

Guided Learning: Compare your paragraph with the one in the Teacher Guide.

Activity 3: The Invention Factory *(Offline)*
Write a presentation for the tour guides at the Invention Factory.

People from all over the country travel to West Orange, New Jersey to visit the Edison National Historic Site. There they can tour Glenmont, home of Thomas Edison, and the Laboratory. Tour guides take visitors through Edison's Invention Factory, where he and his team of inventors cranked out more than 500 inventions. Imagine you have been given the task of writing the text of the presentation given by tour guides at the Invention Factory. The presentation should tell about Thomas Edison, his inventions, and how he came up with them. Use information from the story "The Wizard of Menlo Park" in your presentation. Remember that what you write will be memorized and recited by tour guides.

Your work will be used as the assessment for this lesson. Make sure you've included the most important information from the lesson.

ASSESS
Lesson Assessment: The Wizard of Menlo Park: Thomas Edison *(Online)*
Have an adult review your Invention Factory essay and input the results in the assessment at the end of the lesson.

LEARN
Activity 4. Optional: The Wizard of Menlo Park: Thomas Edison *(Online)*

Lesson Assessment

The Wizard of Menlo Park: Thomas Edison

People from all over the country travel to West Orange, New Jersey to visit the Edison National Historic Site. There they can tour Glenmont, home of Thomas Edison, and the Laboratory. Tour guides take visitors through Edison's Invention Factory, where he and his team of inventors cranked out more than 500 inventions.

Imagine you have been given the task of writing the text of the presentation given by tour guides at the Invention Factory. The presentation should tell about Thomas Edison, his inventions, and how he came up with them. Use information from the story "The Wizard of Menlo Park" in your presentation. Remember that what you write will be memorized and recited by tour guides.

Make sure you've included the most important information from the lesson.

Student Guide
Lesson 4: Alexander Graham Bell and the Telephone

In America, a spirit of invention filled the air in the late 1800s. One of the greatest inventions was the telephone. Alexander Graham Bell was the genius who brought this invention--and many others--to life.

Lesson Objectives

- Explain that the late 1800s was a time of many great inventions in America.
- Describe the telephone as a means of carrying speech over wires, and a major improvement in communication.
- Identify Alexander Graham Bell as the inventor of the telephone.

PREPARE

Approximate lesson time is 60 minutes.

Materials

For the Student

Inventors: A Library of Congress Book by Martin Sandler

pencils, colored, 16 colors or more

poster board

Keywords and Pronunciation

patent : The right to make, use, or sell an invention.

LEARN
Activity 1: Inventor of the Telephone (Offline)

Instructions

Print the Student Guide and follow the instructions.

Get Ready

1. What was Samuel F. B. Morse's famous invention?
2. Thomas Edison began his career as a telegraph operator, but then he became an inventor. What are some of his inventions?
3. As Edison's remarkable bulb lit up American homes, which of his other "inventions" was widely adopted by research and industry?

Guided Learning: Check with an adult for the answers to these questions.

Edison came up with more than one thousand inventions. But he wasn't the only successful inventor. America had inventing fever. Let's read about some other amazing inventors, and another great genius, Alexander Graham Bell.

Read "Hothouse of Activity" (pages 24-27), in Inventors by Martin Sandler.

---

1. Americans came up with many inventions between 1860 and 1890. What are some of the devices they created?
2. The Centennial Exhibition in 1876 celebrated the hundredth anniversary of American independence. Like the Great Exhibition in London years before, it showcased industry--this time, mostly American industry. Elisha Otis was one of the inventors honored there. What did he invent?
3. What did George Westinghouse invent?
4. Who exhibited the telephone at that fair?

Guided Learning: Check with an adult for the answers to these questions.

Read pages 28-33 in Inventors by Martin Sandler.

1. Why was the telephone such an important advance over the telegraph?
2. In addition to making communication faster and easier, how else did the telephone help people?
3. What does the picture on page 30 tell us about how the urban landscaped changed with the telephone?
4. What were some of Alexander Graham Bell's other inventions ?
5. How did George Washington Carver contribute to this age of invention?

Guided Learning: Check with an adult for the answers to these questions.

Show You Know

1. When you think about inventions, how would you describe the period between 1860 and 1890 in America?
2. Who invented the telephone?
3. What was the telephone?
4. How would you describe Alexander Graham Bell?

Guided Learning: Check with an adult for the answers to these questions.

Activity 2: History Journal *(Offline)*

It's time to add another chapter to the story of the past. Follow the directions to complete a new entry in your History Journal.

Turn to a new page in your History Journal. On this page, write a paragraph that tells what the lesson was about.

Begin with a topic sentence that introduces the paragraph. Include at least three sentences that give details about the lesson. End with a concluding sentence. You may use the Show You Know questions to help you get started.

When you have finished, check your work. Make sure you have written complete sentences. Check to make sure you used correct capitalization and punctuation. Date your entry and label it with the lesson title.

Guided Learning: Compare your paragraph with the one in the Teacher Guide.

Activity 3: The Great Age of American Invention *(Offline)*

Create a poster showing some of the inventions featured in the book *Inventors*.

Eureka! The 1800s began an exciting period in American history--an age of invention! Americans demonstrated an inventive spirit that resulted in many inventions. The inventions improved life throughout the world.

Create a poster celebrating America's inventive spirit. Include drawings and descriptions of some of the inventions featured in the book *Inventors*. Choose the inventions that interest you the most.

ASSESS

Lesson Assessment: Alexander Graham Bell and the Telephone *(Offline)*

You will complete an offline assessment covering the main objectives of this lesson. Your learning coach will score this assessment.

Name _____   Date _____

Alexander Graham Bell and the Telephone

Fill in the blanks to complete this paragraph. Use the words and phrases from the Word Box.

The late 1800s was a time of many great ___inventions___ in

America. In 1875, _____ invented the telephone.

The telephone was a major _____ in

_____. It could carry ___speech___

a long distance over ___wires___ .

Word Box

| improvement | Alexander Graham Bell | speech |
| inventions | Samuel Morse | wires | communication |

Student Guide
Lesson 5: Carnegie and Steel

Andrew Carnegie came to the United States as a poor boy. He ended up as the richest man in the world. He also turned steel into a great industry.

Lesson Objectives

- Describe Andrew Carnegie as an industrious Scottish immigrant.
- Explain that Carnegie built the steel industry in America and became one of the wealthiest men of his time.
- Describe steel as an extremely strong metal used to build railroads, buildings, and bridges.

PREPARE

Approximate lesson time is 60 minutes.

Materials

For the Student

📖 The Wonder of Steel

Inventors: A Library of Congress Book by Martin Sandler

LEARN
Activity 1: The Generous Man of Steel *(Online)*

Activity 2: History Journal *(Offline)*

It's time to add another chapter to the story of the past. Follow the directions to complete a new entry in your History Journal.

Turn to a new page in your History Journal. On this page, write a paragraph that tells what the lesson was about.

Begin with a topic sentence that introduces the paragraph. Include at least three sentences that give details about the lesson. End with a concluding sentence. You may use the Show You Know questions to help you get started.

When you have finished, check your work. Make sure you have written in complete sentences. Check to make sure you used correct capitalization and punctuation. Date your entry and label it with the lesson title.

Guided Learning: Compare your paragraph with the one in the Teacher Guide.

Activity 3: The Wonder of Steel *(Offline)*

Read the chapter titled "The Wonder of Steel," pages 34-39, in the book *Inventors.* Then print and complete the Wonder of Steel activity sheet.

Guided Learning: Have an adult check the answers on this sheet.

ASSESS

Lesson Assessment: Carnegie and Steel (*Online*)

You will complete an online assessment covering the main objectives of this lesson. Your assessment will be scored by the computer.

Name _____ Date _____

The Wonder of Steel

Many inventions were not possible until the process of making steel was fully developed. Once steel mills began turning out the extremely strong, durable metal, inventors had a new material at their disposal. In America, the steel industry was built almost single-handedly by Andrew Carnegie, an industrious Scottish immigrant. He went on to become one of the wealthiest men of his time.

1. Steel allowed inventors to design and build large agricultural *an* / *giant* machines. What was a result of this?

   _____

   _____

   _____

2. Steel was the strongest building material of the day. It made possible the construction of skyscrapers and enormous bridges. What effect do you think this had on cities?

   improved the city

   _____

   _____

3. By the end of the nineteenth century (the 1800s), inventions had made life easier for millions of Americans. Now they had a little time for recreation. Businessmen turned to steel to help them create amusements for hardworking Americans. Give two examples of inventions that used steel to create thrilling experiences in the new amusement parks.

   Roller coaster

   ferris wheel

Student Guide
Lesson 6. Optional: Mr. Eiffel Builds a Tower

The French weren't left behind in this "can do" age. To celebrate the one hundredth anniversary of the French Revolution, Gustave Eiffel built a tower a thousand feet tall. It was the tallest building in the world and has become a symbol of France.

Lesson Objectives

- Identify the Eiffel Tower from a set of images, and locate it in Paris, France.
- Describe Gustave Eiffel as the designer of the Eiffel Tower.
- Describe the Eiffel Tower as a symbol of France.
- Name two characteristics of the Eiffel Tower, such as it is made of iron; it is very tall; it has elevators.

PREPARE

Approximate lesson time is 60 minutes.

Materials

For the Student

History Journal

index cards, 4" x 6"

pencils, colored, 16 colors or more

Keywords and Pronunciation

Alexandre-Gustave Eiffel (GOUS-tahv IY-fuhl)

LEARN
Activity 1. Optional: Optional Lesson Instructions *(Online)*

This lesson is OPTIONAL. It is provided for students who seek enrichment or extra practice. You may skip this lesson.

If you choose to skip this lesson, then go to the Plan or Lesson Lists page and mark this lesson "Skipped" in order to proceed to the next lesson in the course.

Activity 2. Optional: A Monument For Paris *(Online)*

Activity 3. Optional: History Journal *(Offline)*

It's time to add another chapter to the story of the past. Follow the directions to complete a new entry in your History Journal.

Turn to a new page in your History Journal. On this page, write a paragraph that tells what the lesson was about.

Begin with a topic sentence that introduces the paragraph. Include at least three sentences that give details about the lesson. End with a concluding sentence. You may use the Show You Know questions to help you get started.

When you have finished, check your work. Make sure you have written in complete sentences. Check to make sure you used correct capitalization and punctuation. Date your entry and label it with the lesson title.

Guided Learning: Compare your paragraph with the one in the Teacher Guide.

Activity 4. Optional: Greetings From the Eiffel Tower *(Offline)*

Imagine you're visiting Paris. Make a postcard with an image and information about the Eiffel Tower. Print the Student Guide for instructions.

1. Use a large index card (4" x 6" or 5" x 7") without lines on one side.
2. On the side without lines, draw the Eiffel Tower. Add color with markers or colored pencils.
3. Divide the other side with a vertical line down the middle.
4. On the right-hand side, write some facts about the Eiffel Tower.
5. On the left-hand side, write a short note to a friend back home.

Activity 5. Optional: Mr. Eiffel Builds a Tower *(Online)*

Student Guide
Lesson 7: Henry Ford Makes Cars Affordable

The invention of the gasoline engine made automobiles practical. But building a car was very costly and time-consuming until Henry Ford set up his Model T factory. His assembly line made cars quickly and cheaply--so the average family could finally afford one!

Lesson Objectives

- Associate Gottlieb Daimler and Karl Benz with the development of the gasoline engine.
- Identify Henry Ford as an American businessman who started assembly-line production of automobiles.
- Identify the Model T as a kind of car.
- Explain that Ford's assembly line factory made production faster and cheaper.

PREPARE

Approximate lesson time is 60 minutes.

Materials
> For the Student
>> History Journal
>> Model T: How Henry Ford Built a Legend by David Weitzman

Keywords and Pronunciation
Gottlieb Daimler (GAHT-leeb DIYM-lur)
Karl Benz (bents)

LEARN
Activity 1: Henry Ford and the Model T *(Online)*

Activity 2: History Journal *(Offline)*

It's time to add another chapter to the story of the past. Follow the directions to complete a new entry in your History Journal.

Turn to a new page in your History Journal. On this page, write a paragraph that tells what the lesson was about.

Begin with a topic sentence that introduces the paragraph. Include at least three sentences that give details about the lesson. End with a concluding sentence. You may use the Show You Know questions to help you get started.

When you have finished, check your work. Make sure you have written in complete sentences. Check to make sure you used correct capitalization and punctuation. Date your entry and label it with the lesson title.

Guided Learning: Compare your paragraph with the one in the Teacher Guide.

Activity 3: Ford is Hiring! *(Offline)*

It's 1915. Ford is hiring. Write a newspaper advertisement to recruit workers for Henry Ford's factory. Read the Student Guide for directions to complete this activity.

Create a newspaper advertisement to recruit workers for Henry Ford's automobile factory. You might want to include some, or all, of the following information:

- The name of the particular car being made at the factory
- The method of production used at the factory
- The advantages of working at the Ford Motor Company

ASSESS

Lesson Assessment: Henry Ford Makes Cars Affordable *(Online)*

You will complete an online assessment covering the main objectives of this lesson. Your assessment will be scored by the computer.

LEARN

Activity 4. Optional: Henry Ford Makes Cars Affordable *(Offline)*

Student Guide
Lesson 8: Marconi and the Radio

Thanks to the telegraph and the telephone, people could send messages over long distances in no time. But both inventions needed wires to carry a signal from place to place. Was there a way to send messages without wires? Guglielmo Marconi answered that question.

Lesson Objectives
- Describe the radio as a wireless form of communication.
- Identify Marconi as the first to send wireless signals through the air and across the Atlantic Ocean.
- Explain that the first radios were used by sinking ships to call for help.

PREPARE

Approximate lesson time is 60 minutes.

Materials
> For the Student
>> History Journal

Keywords and Pronunciation
Enrico Caruso (ayn-REE-koh kah-ROO-soh)
Guglielmo Marconi (gool-YEL-moh mahr-KOH-nee)

LEARN
Activity 1: Marconi: The Father of Radio *(Online)*

Activity 2: History Journal *(Offline)*
It's time to add another chapter to the story of the past. Follow the directions to complete a new entry in your History Journal.

Turn to a new page in your History Journal. On this page, write a paragraph that tells what the lesson was about.

Begin with a topic sentence that introduces the paragraph. Include at least three sentences that give details about the lesson. End with a concluding sentence. You may use the Show You Know questions to help you get started.

When you have finished, check your work. Make sure you have written in complete sentences. Check to make sure you used correct capitalization and punctuation. Date your entry and label it with the lesson title.

Guided Learning: Compare your paragraph with the one in the Teacher Guide.

Activity 3: Marconi's Acceptance Speech *(Offline)*

Write the speech Marconi might have given when he received an award in 1909.

The 1909 Nobel Prize in Physics was awarded jointly to Guglielmo Marconi and Karl Ferdinand Braun, "in recognition of their contributions to the development of wireless telegraphy." Braun was experimenting with radio in Germany in the years following Marconi's transmission of radio signals across the Atlantic. Write Marconi's acceptance speech for the award he received in 1909. Use information from the lesson to help you write the speech.

ASSESS

Lesson Assessment: Marconi and the Radio *(Online)*

You will complete an online assessment covering the main objectives of this lesson. Your assessment will be scored by the computer.

LEARN

Activity 4. Optional: Marconi and the Radio *(Online)*

Student Guide
Lesson 9: First in Flight: Orville and Wilbur Wright

Could a man fly? By the late 1800s many inventors were trying to soar. Two clever brothers did it! Orville and Wilbur Wright built a plane and flew the first successful flight in Kitty Hawk, North Carolina, in 1903.

Lesson Objectives

- Describe Orville and Wilbur Wright as the inventors of the first successful airplane.
- State that the first successful flight occurred at Kitty Hawk, North Carolina.
- Explain that after the Wrights' invention, more and more pilots took to the skies.

PREPARE

Approximate lesson time is 60 minutes.

Materials

For the Student

History Journal

The Wright Brothers in Time activity sheet

Pioneers of the Air by Molly Burkett

Keywords and Pronunciation

Aviation : The science of flying; air travel.

LEARN
Activity 1: Meet the Wright Brothers (Offline)
Instructions
Print the Student Guide and follow the instructions.

Get Ready
1. Alexander Graham Bell figured out how to send speech through wires. What was his invention?
2. Thomas Edison brightened American homes. What did he invent?
3. Which two Germans invented the gas engine for the automobile?
4. Which American figured out a way to produce automobiles cheaply?
5. Which resourceful Italian invented the first "wireless telegraph," or radio?
6. How was the radio used at first?

Guided Learning: Check with an adult for the answers to these questions.

Reach for the sky! That seemed to be the slogan of this "can-do" age. Aim high. Shoot for the stars. The number of inventions soared in the late 1800s. The telegraph, telephone, lightbulb, steel, radio, automobile-- the list goes on and on. But some bold inventors wanted to reach even higher. They wanted to soar IN the sky, not just reach for it. *Aviation*, the science of flying, was born. Today we'll learn about some pioneers of air travel.

Read pages 74 to 76 in Inventors by Martin Sandler.

1. What were some of the early devices that men such as Du Temple, Ader, Maxim, and Langley tested to learn about flying?
2. What happened on December 17, 1903?
3. Where did they launch their flight?
4. What was the profession of Orville and Wilbur Wright?
5. How long did the first flight last and how far did the airplane travel?

Read pages 77 to 80 in *Inventors* by Martin Sandler.

1. How did the Wright brothers prove their flight was not a piece of luck?
2. How long did the longest flight that day last?
3. The Wright brothers launched their first flight in 1903. By 1909 how far could one of their planes fly?
4. Who made flying popular in the 1910s?
5. A great World War broke out in 1914. You'll study that soon. What effect did World War I have on aviation?

Guided Learning: Check with an adult for the answers to these questions.

In 1903 at Kitty Hawk, North Carolina, a new age was born. This age of aviation continues today. Planes rush people, mail, cargo, food, and medicine to places far away. If you hop on a plane today, the pilot may tell you you're flying at 500 miles per hour. There are planes that fly even faster. Some fly faster than the speed of sound. That's about 760 miles per hour!

Reach for the sky? Orville and Wilbur Wright did. And they got there.

Show You Know

1. Why are Orville and Wilbur Wright famous?
2. Where did they make their famous first flight?
3. After that first flight, were the Wright Brothers the only ones to keep flying?

Guided Learning: Check with an adult for the answers to these questions.

Activity 2: History Journal *(Offline)*

It's time to add another chapter to the story of the past. Follow the directions to complete a new entry in your History Journal.

Turn to a new page in your History Journal. Answer the following questions in complete sentences. An adult will check your answers and use them as the assessment for today's lesson.

Date your entry and label it with the lesson title.

1. Who were the inventors of the first successful airplane?
2. Where did their first successful flight occur?
3. What happened in aviation after the Wrights' invention?

Activity 3: The Wright Brothers in Time *(Offline)*

Print and complete the Wright Brothers in Time activity sheet. Place the complete activity sheet in your History Journal.

Activity 4: First in Flight: Orville and Wilbur Wright *(Offline)*

The Wright brothers were pioneers of the air. Read about them and other aviation pioneers in *Pioneers of the Air*, by Molly Burkett (Barrons Juveniles, 1998).

ASSESS

Lesson Assessment: First in Flight: Orville and Wilbur Wright (*Online*)

Have an adult review your answers to your History Journal entry and input the results online.

Name _____   Date _____

The Wright Brothers in Time

Orville and Wilbur Wright were the inventors of the first successful airplane. Their first successful flight occurred at Kitty Hawk, North Carolina. Soon, more and more pilots began taking to the skies.

On the map below, draw a symbol of the Wright brothers' first plane in the state of North Carolina.

The Wright Brothers in Time

Time Line of Inventions and Innovations

On a sheet of construction paper, create a time line of the following inventions and innovations.
· telephone
· human controlled, powered flight
· light bulb
· telegraph
· mass production of the automobile

On the time line, include the following information for each invention or innovation:
· name of invention or innovation
· year invented (or year innovation was introduced)
· inventor(s) or innovator(s)
· a simple drawing of the invention or innovation

Name _____   Date _____

Lesson Assessment

First in Flight: Orville and Wilbur Wright

Your student was asked the following questions in the Lesson's History Journal entry. Evaluate your student's responses in the activity and input the results online.

1. Who were the inventors of the first successful airplane?

2. Where did their first successful flight occur?

3. What happened in aviation after the Wrights' invention?

Student Guide
Lesson 10: The Panama Canal

Could human beings connect two oceans? Yes! The Panama Canal connected the Atlantic and Pacific Oceans. With the canal, ships could travel from California to New York more quickly. The Panama Canal was one of the greatest engineering feats of all time.

Lesson Objectives

- Locate the Isthmus of Panama on a map.
- Describe the Panama Canal as a waterway connecting the Atlantic and Pacific Oceans.
- Explain that Americans wanted to build the canal to shorten a ship's travel time between the east and west coasts of the United States.
- Name two obstacles the canal builders had to overcome, such as yellow fever, heat, construction of locks, and landslides.

PREPARE

Approximate lesson time is 60 minutes.

Materials

For the Student

📇 Map of Panama

map, world

History Journal

Keywords and Pronunciation

Culebra (koo-LAY-brah)

isthmus (IS-muhs) : A narrow strip of land connecting two larger land areas.

locks : Compartments of water in a canal; the water level in a lock can be raised or lowered to allow a ship to pass through the canal.

William Gorgas (GOR-gas)

LEARN
Activity 1: Connecting Two Oceans *(Online)*
Instructions
Print the Panama map and start the lesson.

Activity 2: History Journal *(Offline)*

It's time to add another chapter to the story of the past. Follow the directions to complete a new entry in your History Journal.

Turn to a new page in your History Journal. On this page, write a paragraph that tells what the lesson was about.

Begin with a topic sentence that introduces the paragraph. Include at least three sentences that give details about the lesson. End with a concluding sentence. You may use the Show You Know questions to help you get started.

When you have finished, check your work. Make sure you have written in complete sentences. Check to make sure you used correct capitalization and punctuation. Date your entry and label it with the lesson title.

Guided Learning: Compare your paragraph with the one in the Teacher Guide.

ASSESS

Lesson Assessment: The Panama Canal *(Offline)*

You will complete an online assessment covering the main objectives of this lesson. Your assessment will be scored by the computer.

LEARN

Activity 3: The Panama Canal *(Online)*

Explore a wealth of photographs and documents concerning the Panama Canal.

Panama

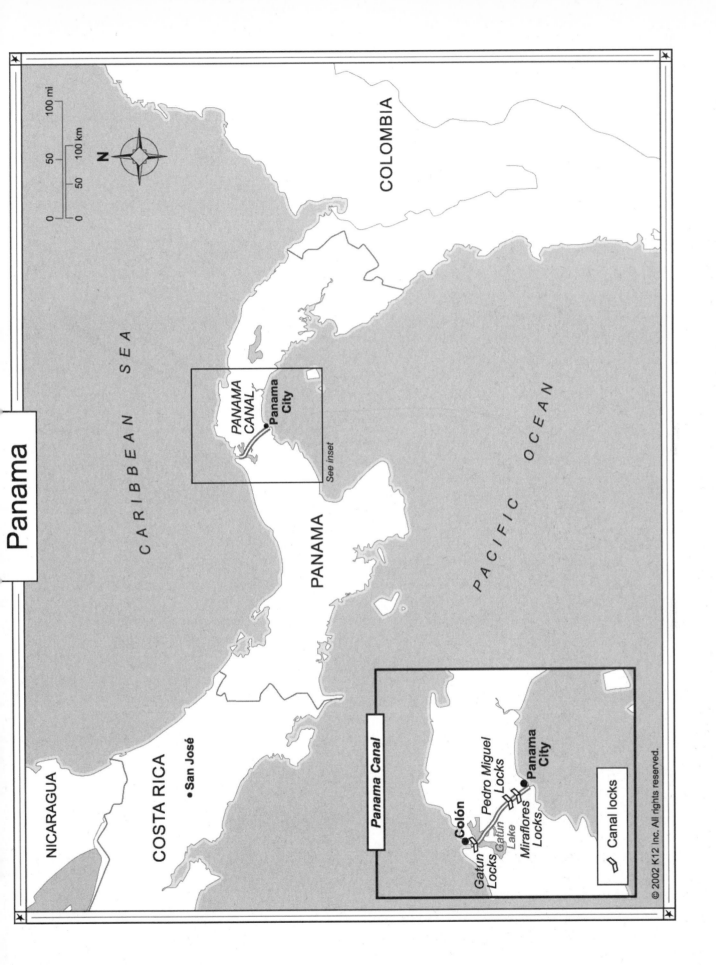

NICARAGUA

COSTA RICA

• San José

COLOMBIA

CARIBBEAN SEA

PANAMA

PACIFIC OCEAN

PANAMA CANAL

Panama City

See inset

N

100 mi
50
0

100 km
50
0

Panama Canal

Colón

Gatún Locks

Gatún Lake

Pedro Miguel Locks

Miraflores Locks

Panama City

Canal locks

Student Guide
Lesson 11: Unit Review and Assessment

You've completed this unit, and now it's time to review what you've learned and take the unit assessment.

Lesson Objectives

- Demonstrate mastery of important knowledge and skills in this unit.
- Explain that Pasteur studied bacteria, and learned that it could sour food and spread disease.
- Describe pasteurization as a process of using heat to kill bacteria.
- Describe the Morse code as a series of clicks and pauses used to transmit messages.
- Describe Edison as one of the greatest inventors of all time.
- Name the electric lightbulb as one of his inventions.
- Explain that Edison's "Invention Factory" became a model for industrial research laboratories.
- Describe Andrew Carnegie as an industrious Scottish immigrant.
- Explain that Carnegie built the steel industry in America and became one of the wealthiest men of his time.
- Associate Gottlieb Daimler and Karl Benz with the development of the gasoline engine.
- Explain that Ford's assembly line factory made production faster and cheaper.
- Describe the radio as a wireless form of communication.
- Identify Marconi as the first to send wireless signals through the air and across the Atlantic Ocean.
- Describe Orville and Wilbur Wright as the inventors of the first successful airplane.
- State that the first successful flight occurred at Kitty Hawk, North Carolina.
- Describe the Panama Canal as a waterway connecting the Atlantic and Pacific Oceans.
- Name two obstacles the canal builders had to overcome, such as yellow fever, heat, construction of locks, and landslides.
- Identify Alexander Graham Bell as the inventor of the telephone.
- Identify some of the key innovators of the period (Pasteur, Samuel B. Morse, Thomas Edison, Alexander Graham Bell, Andrew Carnegie, Gustave Eiffel, Daimler and Benz, Henry Ford, Guglielmo Marconi, Orville and Wilbur Wright).
- Identify some of the major inventions, and innovations of the period (pasteurization, development of the telegraph, electric light, the telephone, steel industry, automobile, automobile factory, radio, airplanes, the Panama Canal).

PREPARE

Approximate lesson time is 60 minutes.

LEARN
Activity 1: Can Do! An Age of Breakthroughs and Enterprise *(Offline)*

We've covered a lot, and now it's time to take a look back. Here's what you should remember about the Age of Breakthroughs and Enterprise.

Every so often, human history seems to take a great leap forward. Suddenly people are able to do things they have never done before. They see their world in a whole new light.
The late nineteenth and early twentieth centuries were such a time. In Europe and in the United States, people had invention fever. They sped up communication and transportation. They figured out new ways to cure diseases and to link the seas. It was an age of confidence. "Can do!" was the attitude. "We can figure it out. We can make it happen." Great optimism marked the age, and people went further than ever before. Let's remember some of their achievements.

We learned about a French scientist who helped his countrymen solve a problem. Their wine was spoiling. He discovered that bacteria were spoiling the wine. What was his name? [1]
Pasteur soon realized that harmful bacteria spoil other foods, too, and even cause human diseases. He came up with a process for heating wine and killing the harmful bacteria. What was that process called? [2]
Can you think of ways we use pasteurization today? [3]
Samuel Morse wasn't interested in bacteria. But he was interested in the speedy delivery of information--about bacteria and about everything else. He invented a way to send information quickly over wires using electric pulses. What was his invention called? [4]
Morse even invented a special code to send those messages using clicks and pauses. What do we call that code? [5]

Some of America's greatest inventors began their careers in Morse's footsteps, as telegraph operators. One of them made an improved telegraph. Then he made then an electric vote counter, then a phonograph. He did much of his work in Menlo Park, New Jersey. Who was that "Wizard of Menlo Park"? [6]
Thomas Alva Edison gave us many inventions, but one lights up our lives even now. What is it? [7]
Edison built an "invention factory" that helped him come up with many inventions and products. What was his "invention factory"? [8]
The telegraph, phonograph, electric light--could it get any better? Alexander Graham Bell thought so. He said, "If we can send electric pulses through wires, maybe we can start sending human voices over wires, too." He invented a device to do just that. What did Bell invent? [9]

Then an Italian inventor named Marconi thought it would be great to send electric pulses and human voices without wires. Nobody thought much of his "wireless" at first, but the British did. They helped him set up the first "wireless" company. What did Marconi invent? [10]
Improvements in medicine and communications were just one part of this age of invention. Don't forget about the great improvements in building. One man, a Scottish immigrant to America, made a lot of building possible. His name was Andrew Carnegie. How did he help? [11]
Why did steel turn out to be such an important material? [12]
Suddenly people could build very long bridges and really tall buildings. One man got busy on a very tall tower in Paris. Do you remember his name? [13]

The Eiffel Tower became the symbol of France. Do you remember another famous structure Eiffel worked on? (Hint: It now stands in New York Harbor and is a famous symbol of America.) [14]

Statues, buildings, and bridges weren't the only things steel made possible. When two Germans named Daimler and Benz invented a gas-powered automobile, an American figured out how to make it faster and cheaper. He used steel parts. He started his own automobile factory. His most famous car was the Model T. Who was that man? [15]

Soon cars were cheap. People were riding around in automobiles and wishing crazy things. Wishing they could even fly! "Well, why not?" said two brothers. They tinkered around with ideas about flying in their bicycle shop in Dayton, Ohio. They tested their ideas at Kitty Hawk, North Carolina. Who were those brothers? [16] What did Orville and Wilbur Wright invent? [17]

Now, if you could cross the land by train and car, and soar through the air in a plane, wasn't just about anything possible? Could human beings dig through land and link the oceans? In the early 1900s, Americans gave it try. They wanted to make it faster and easier to travel between two oceans. Which two oceans did they want to unite? [18]

What was the name of the great canal that linked those two oceans? [19]

Whew! What an age! By the early 1900s, the world felt like a smaller place. Information traveled fast. People traveled fast. All sorts of machines and devices were making the world more exciting and more pleasant. Imagine how much improved life seemed when you could read by electric light at night or call your faraway grandmother on the telephone. "Can do!" said people of the age. Was there anything humans couldn't do? The frontiers to the future seemed wide open.

[1] Louis Pasteur

[2] pasteurization

[3] in milk, cheese, and other foods

[4] the telegraph

[5] Morse code

[6] Thomas Edison

[7] the electric light bulb

[8] Possible answers: a laboratory where lots of assistants worked on inventions together; a place where scientists worked with Edison to test, improve, and invent things.

[9] the telephone

[10] the wireless telegraph, or the radio

[11] He started the steel industry in America.

[12] It is very strong and lighter than iron.

[13] Gustave Eiffel

[14] Eiffel made the skeleton for the Statue of Liberty.

[15] Henry Ford

[16] Orville and Wilbur Wright

[17] the first airplane

[18] the Atlantic and the Pacific

[19] the Panama Canal

Activity 2: Online Interactive Review *(Online)*

ASSESS

Unit Assessment: Can Do! An Age of Breakthroughs and Enterprise *(Offline)*

Complete an offline Unit Assessment. Your learning coach will score this part of the Assessment.

Name _____   Date _____ 5/21/15

Can Do! An Age of Breakthroughs and Enterprise

Read each question and its answer choices. Fill in the bubble in front of the best answer.

1. The telegraph transmitted message through:

    ⓐ   water, using a system of canals

    ⓑ   wires, using a system of clicks and pauses

    ⓒ   air, using a highly developed radio

    ⓓ   telephone lines, using cable technology

2. Which important French scientist discovered that harmful bacteria spoil certain foods?

    ⓐ   Gustave Eiffel

    ⓑ   Louis Pasteur

    ⓒ   Ferdinand de Lesseps

    ⓓ   Baron de Coubertin

3. That French scientist figured out a way to:

    ⓐ   keep wine from souring by using steel casks

    ⓑ   kill bacteria by heating it

    ⓒ   avoid problems by rotating vineyards

    ⓓ   store wine at cool temperatures

4. Both Thomas Edison and Andrew Carnegie worked as telegraph operators. That meant they had to learn:

   ⓐ pasteurization

   ⓑ to use arc lights

   ⓒ radio frequencies

   ⓓ Morse Code

5. Carnegie worked in the railroad industry, but how did Andrew Carnegie make his fortune?

   ⓐ sewing machines

   ⓑ steel plants

   ⓒ telephone

   ⓓ typewriters

6. The "Wizard of Menlo Park" was one of the greatest inventors of all time. His most famous invention was the electric lightbulb. Who was the "Wizard of Menlo Park"?

   ⓐ Alexander Graham Bell

   ⓑ Thomas Edison

   ⓒ Samuel Morse

   ⓓ Andrew Carnegie

7. What was one reason Thomas Edison was so productive?

    ⓐ He had an automated assembly line that sped up production of his inventions.

    ⓑ He used hundreds of typewriters and electric telegraphs inside his laboratories.

    ⓒ He had a system of note-taking that was impossible for other businessmen to read.

    ⓓ He had an "invention factory" that became a model for research laboratories.

8. Which famous Scottish immigrant to America invented the telephone?

    ⓐ Andrew Carnegie

    ⓑ Alexander Graham Bell

    ⓒ Henry Ford

    ⓓ Guglielmo Marconi

9. Which of the following "headlines" describes the accomplishment of the Wright brothers?

    ⓐ First in Flight

    ⓑ More Model Ts

    ⓒ Engineers of the Eiffel

    ⓓ Pioneers in Sound

10. This industrious Scottish immigrant ended up giving away the fortune he made in the steel industry. Who was he?

    ⓐ Alexander Graham Bell

    ⓑ James Hargreaves

    ⓒ Andrew Carnegie

    ⓓ Louis Pasteur

11. Where was the first successful airplane flight?

(a) Detroit, Michigan

(b) Paris, France

(c) Kitty Hawk, North Carolina

(d) Menlo Park, New Jersey

12. A great engineering triumph connected the Atlantic and Pacific Oceans. What was that waterway called?

(a) the Suez Canal

(b) the Panama Canal

(c) the Erie Canal

(d) the Grand Canal

13. Guglielmo Marconi tried to get someone to fund his invention in Italy, but no one was interested. He ended up going to England for help. What did he invent?

(a) electric vote counter

(b) radio

(c) telephone

(d) telegraph

14. Which invention of Gottlieb Daimler and Karl Benz encouraged automobile production?

(a) gas engine

(b) assembly line

(c) rapid steel production

(d) Model T

15. What were some of the dangers faced by workers on the Panama Canal?

   (a)   cold, pneumonia, harsh winters

   (b)   poor lighting and ventilation

   (c)   angry resentment of Panamanians

   (d)   malaria, yellow fever, rockslides

16. Henry Ford made it possible for many people to own cars. How did he accomplish that?

   (a)   He sold cars at less than it cost him to produce them.

   (b)   His efficient assembly line made cars a lot cheaper to produce.

   (c)   He invented the gas engine, which made cars light and more affordable.

   (d)   His many factories employed lots of people who bought cheap cars.

17. What is the correct chronological order for these important inventions?

   (a)   telephone, radio, telegraph, airplane

   (b)   airplane, automobile, radio, lightbulb

   (c)   radio, telephone, telegraph, Model T

   (d)   telegraph, lightbulb, airplane, Model T

18-23. A sixty-point essay question:

This unit was called "Can-do!" It described the spirit of the late nineteenth and early twentieth centuries. Write a paragraph about this age of invention and enterprise. Start with the topic sentence:

In the late 1800s and early 1900s people were full of new ideas and they made many wonderful advances.

Include the following:

- Tell about one advance in biology and the person who made it.
- Tell about one advance in communication and the person who invented it.
- Tell about one advance in transportation and the person who made it possible.

_____

_____

_____

_____

_____

_____

_____

_____

_____

_____

_____

_____

Student Guide
Lesson 1: The Great War Begins

The early part of the twentieth century was an era of great ups and downs -- mostly downs: A long deadly war in Europe was followed by a few roaring good years in the U.S.A. In Russia a cruel dictator rose to power. All over the world economies began to crumble. It was a time that tested people's courage and perseverance.

Few people expected a terrible world war in 1914. But war came, and it involved many countries. Could the nations of the world fight each other in a short war? In 1914, the thinking was "Can do!" The result was a disaster.

Lesson Objectives

- Recognize the term "the Great War" was used at the time to describe World War I.
- Recognize the slogans "make the world safe for democracy" and "the war to end all wars" as slogans that brought the United States into World War I.
- Describe World War I as a long and deadly war involving many nations and great destruction.
- Explain that trench warfare was characteristic of World War I.
- Explain that American entry into World War I turned the tide of victory.
- Explain that the peace that followed the war left many people dissatisfied.
- Describe the Russian Revolution as one that involved the overthrow of the czar and the triumph of Communism.
- Describe the 1920s in the United States as a period of economic growth and many social changes.
- Describe the Great Depression as a world-wide economic depression in the 1930s.
- Name some of the key figures of the period from 1914 to 1930 (Woodrow Wilson, Vladmir Lenin, Josef Stalin, Alice Paul, Charles Lindbergh, Alexander Fleming, Franklin Delano Roosevelt).
- Name some of the key events, phrases, and advances of the period between 1914 and 1930 (World War I, League of Nations, Russian Revolution, Roaring Twenties, women's suffrage, solo flight across the Atlantic, discovery of penicillin, the Great Depression).
- Explain that nationalism and military alliances triggered the First World War.
- Explain that advances in technology contributed to a long and deadly war.
- Describe the nations of Europe as confident that the war would be short.
- State that the "the Great War" was the term used to describe World War I.

PREPARE

Approximate lesson time is 60 minutes.

Materials

For the Student

- Map of Europe on the eve of World War I, 1914
- Alliances

Keywords and Pronunciation

alliance (uh-LIY-uhnts) : An agreement between partners; an agreement between countries to help each other.

LEARN

Activity 1: The Powder Keg of Europe *(Online)*

In 1914, Europe seemed to explode as war broke out. Find out why people came to call this war the Great War.

Activity 2: History Journal *(Offline)*

It's time to add another chapter to the story of the past. Follow the directions to complete a new entry in your History Journal.

Turn to a new page in your History Journal. Write a paragraph that tells what the lesson was about. Begin with a topic sentence that introduces the paragraph. Include at least three sentences that give details about the lesson. End with a concluding sentence. You may use the Show You Know questions to help you get started.

When you have finished, check your work. Make sure you have written in complete sentences. Check to make sure you used correct capitalization and punctuation. Date your entry and label it with the lesson title.

Guided Learning: Compare your paragraph with the one in the Teacher Guide.

Activity 3: Alliances *(Offline)*

Print and complete the Alliances activity sheet. You'll need the map of Europe 1914 (Pre WWI) that you used during the lesson.

ASSESS

Lesson Assessment: The Great War Begins (*Online*)

You will complete an online assessment covering the main objectives of this lesson. Your assessment will be scored by the computer.

Europe on the eve of World War I, 1914

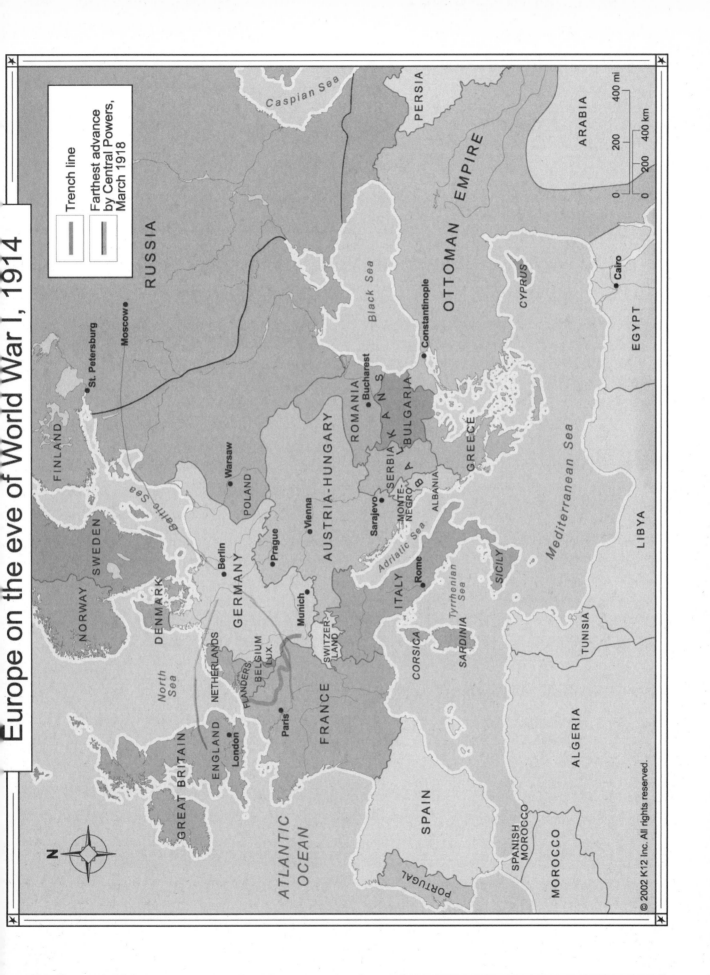

Legend:
- Trench line
- Farthest advance by Central Powers, March 1918

400 mi
400 km
0 200
0 200

Labels on map:

Caspian Sea
PERSIA
ARABIA
RUSSIA
OTTOMAN EMPIRE
Moscow
St. Petersburg
FINLAND
Black Sea
Constantinople
Cairo
EGYPT
CYPRUS
SWEDEN
NORWAY
Warsaw
POLAND
Vienna
Prague
AUSTRIA-HUNGARY
ROMANIA
Bucharest
B A L K A N S
SERBIA
BULGARIA
MONTE-NEGRO
ALBANIA
Sarajevo
GREECE
Mediterranean Sea
LIBYA
Baltic Sea
Berlin
GERMANY
DENMARK
Munich
SWITZER-LAND
Adriatic Sea
ITALY
Rome
Tyrrhenian Sea
SICILY
SARDINIA
CORSICA
TUNISIA
NETHERLANDS
BELGIUM
LUX.
FLANDERS
North Sea
GREAT BRITAIN
ENGLAND
London
FRANCE
Paris
ATLANTIC OCEAN
SPAIN
PORTUGAL
SPANISH MOROCCO
MOROCCO
ALGERIA

N

Name _____   Date _____

Alliances

In the early 1900s, European countries began to fear their neighbors. To protect themselves, they began to form *alliances*.

1. On the map on the following page, color Great Britain, France, and Russia green. These three countries formed an alliance that came to be known as

    _____ .

2. Now color Germany, Austria-Hungary, and the Ottoman Empire red. These powers formed an alliance called the

    _____   _____ .

3. In 1914, the *powder keg* was lit. The location was a peninsula in southeastern Europe. It was home to many different nations.

    The region is called the _____. Color this region yellow.

4. The war that resulted was called "the _____ _____."

    Although many thought it would be short, it turned out to be a

    _____ war.

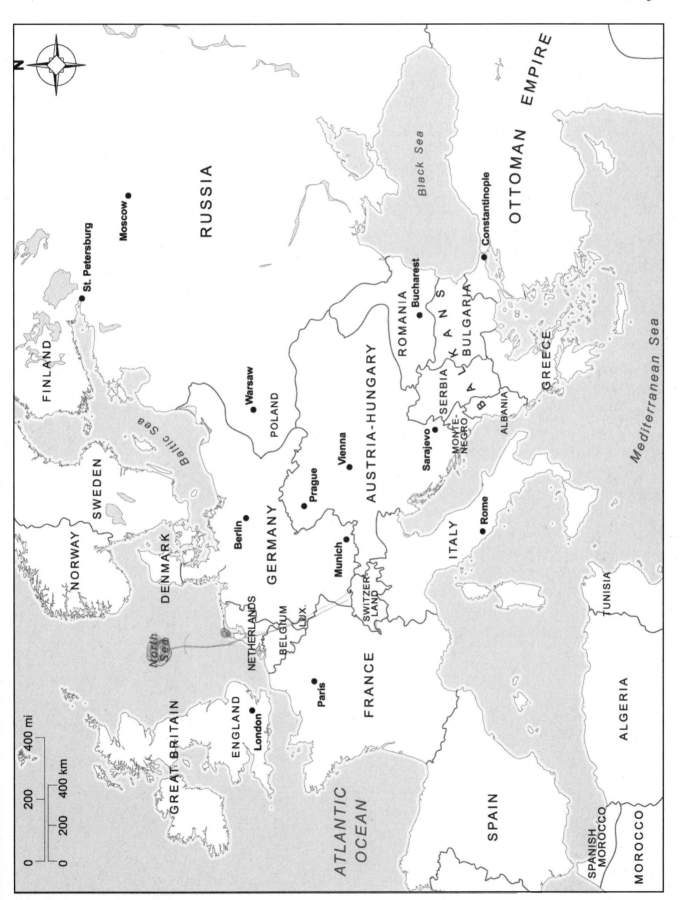

Student Guide
Lesson 2: In Flanders Fields

A terrible war raged for four years on two fronts. Soldiers experienced the horrors of trench warfare, poison gas attacks, lice, disease, and death. One Canadian doctor wrote a famous poem expressing hope that they would not die in vain.

Lesson Objectives

- Explain that the Great War became a very long and deadly war.
- Describe World War I as fought on eastern and western fronts.
- Name two characteristics of trench warfare on the western front.
- Explain that the poem "In Flanders Fields" expressed the hope that the soldiers would not die in vain.

PREPARE

Approximate lesson time is 60 minutes.

Materials

For the Student

- 🖥 Map of Europe on the eve of World War I, 1914
- 🖥 The Tragedy of War

Keywords and Pronunciation

front : In war, a line of battle; an area where enemy armies face each other.

John McCrae (muh-KRAY)

trench : A long cut in the ground; a ditch.

LEARN
Activity 1: A Long War *(Online)*

Read about a poem written during World War I that captures not only the sadness of war but also the love of life and the belief in the cause the soldiers were fighting for.

Activity 2: History Journal *(Offline)*

It's time to add another chapter to the story of the past. Follow the directions to complete a new entry in your History Journal.

Activity 3: A Long and Deadly War *(Offline)*

Make a bar graph to compare casualties from the Great War with those from previous wars.

World War I was a very deadly conflict. Nobody was ready for the devastation it caused. The last large-scale war Europeans had fought were the Napoleonic Wars in the early 1800s. At that time, it was estimated that 2 million soldiers had been killed.

The American Civil War was also a deadly conflict. It is estimated that about 600,000 soldiers died during that war.

Now look at the figures for World War I:

Germany	1,773,700
Russia	1,700,000
France	1,375,800
Austria-Hungary	1,200,000
Great Britain	908,371
Italy	650,000
Turkey	325,000
United States	126,000
Serbia	45,000
Total	**8,103,871 (more than 8 million soldiers)**

Print the Tragedy of War activity sheet. Follow the directions to make a bar graph that compares the casualties from the three wars mentioned above.

ASSESS

Lesson Assessment: In Flanders Fields (*Online*)

You will complete an online assessment covering the main objectives of this lesson. Your assessment will be scored by the computer.

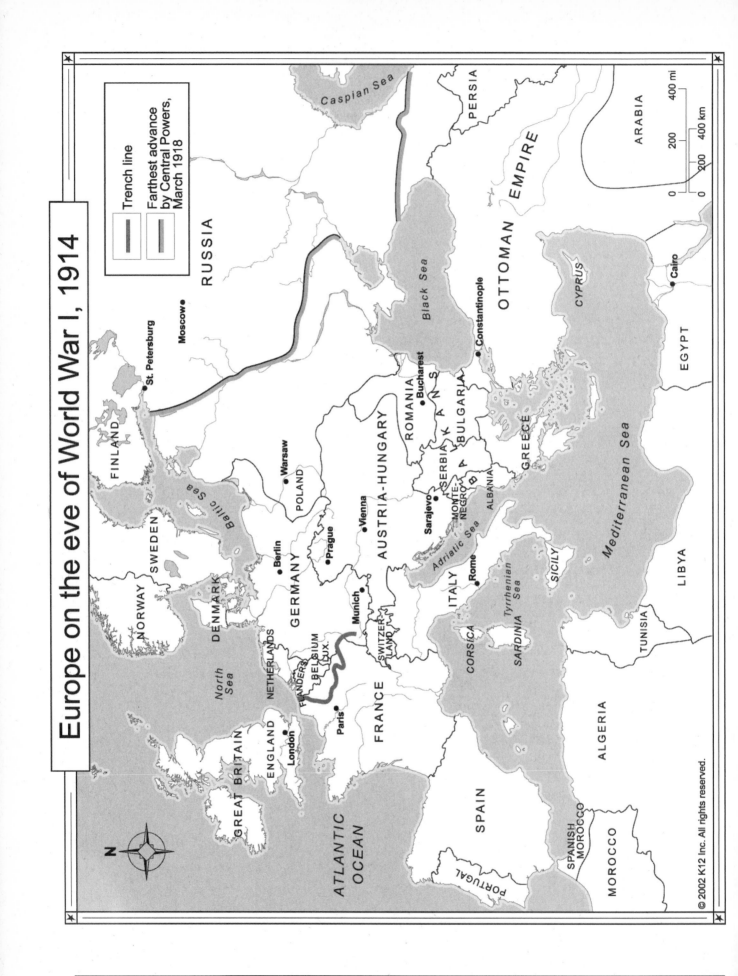

Europe on the eve of World War I, 1914

Legend:
- Trench line
- Farthest advance by Central Powers, March 1918

RUSSIA

Caspian Sea

PERSIA

ARABIA

400 mi
400 km

OTTOMAN EMPIRE

CYPRUS

Cairo

EGYPT

Black Sea

Constantinople

Bucharest

ROMANIA

BULGARIA

B A L K A N S

SERBIA

MONTE-NEGRO

ALBANIA

GREECE

Sarajevo

Mediterranean Sea

LIBYA

Adriatic Sea

Rome

ITALY

SICILY

Tyrrhenian Sea

SARDINIA

CORSICA

TUNISIA

ALGERIA

SPAIN

PORTUGAL

SPANISH MOROCCO

MOROCCO

St. Petersburg

Moscow

FINLAND

SWEDEN

NORWAY

Baltic Sea

Warsaw

POLAND

Vienna

AUSTRIA-HUNGARY

Prague

Berlin

GERMANY

DENMARK

North Sea

NETHERLANDS

BELGIUM

LUX.

FLANDERS

Munich

SWITZER-LAND

Paris

FRANCE

GREAT BRITAIN

ENGLAND

London

ATLANTIC OCEAN

N

Name _____   Date _____

The Tragedy of War

Complete the bar graph below to compare casualties from three conflicts: the Napoleonic Wars, the American Civil War, and the Great War.

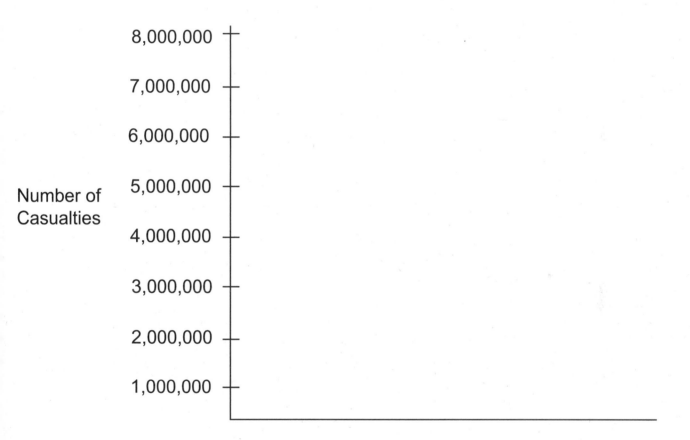

Casualties for Three Conflicts

Student Guide
Lesson 3: Lafayette, We Are Here!

George Washington said Americans should stay out of European wars, and Americans agreed. But in 1917 things changed. The United States entered World War I on the side of the Allies. Americans wanted to "make the world safe for democracy." American troops made all the difference. The Allies won the Great War.

Lesson Objectives

- Explain that since Washington's Farewell Address, the United States had stayed out of European wars.
- Identify Woodrow Wilson as president of the United States during World War I.
- Recognize that "make the world safe for democracy" was a United States slogan in World War I and a reason for entering the war.
- State that the arrival of U.S. troops in Europe helped the Allies begin to win the war.

PREPARE

Approximate lesson time is 60 minutes.

Materials

For the Student

🖥 Americans Over There

poster board

Keywords and Pronunciation

Saint-Nazaire (sen-nah-ZEHR)

LEARN
Activity 1: Americans Over There *(Online)*

Activity 2: History Journal *(Offline)*

It's time to add another chapter to the story of the past. Follow the directions to complete a new entry in your History Journal.

Turn to a new page in your History Journal. On this page, write a paragraph that tells what the lesson was about.

Begin with a topic sentence that introduces the paragraph. Include at least three sentences that give details about the lesson. End with a concluding sentence. You may use the Show You Know questions to help you get started.

When you have finished, check your work. Make sure you have written in complete sentences. Check to make sure you used correct capitalization and punctuation. Date your entry and label it with the lesson title.

Guided Learning: Compare your paragraph with the one in the Teacher Guide.

Activity 3: Newspaper Headlines (Offline)

Create a poster of newspaper headlines from the Great War.

In this lesson, a New York reporter was sending stories about the U.S. Army in Europe. Many reporters were writing stories about the Great War. The newspapers of the day were full of headlines and articles about this long and deadly war.

Come up with at least five headlines that might have appeared in newspapers in the United States during this time. Use a word processor to type your headlines. Use a font like Times New Roman, in a large size.

Print the headlines, cut them out, and attach them to a sheet of poster board. Add a descriptive title to your poster.

If you're having trouble thinking of headlines, reread the lesson.

ASSESS

Lesson Assessment: Lafayette, We Are Here! (Online)

You will complete an online assessment covering the main objectives of this lesson. Your assessment will be scored by the computer.

LEARN

Activity 4. Optional: Lafayette, We Are Here! (Offline)

Do some research to find out why American soldiers stopped at the tomb of General Lafayette to pay their respects.

In the story "Lafayette, We Are Here!" an American officer places a wreath of pink and white roses in front of General Lafayette's tomb. Another officer steps forward, salutes, and says, "Lafayette, we are here!"

What was the big deal about Lafayette? Do a little research on the Marquis de Lafayette to find out. Use a variety of reference materials to learn about his role in the American Revolution. Why do Americans respect him so much?

Europe on the eve of World War I, 1914

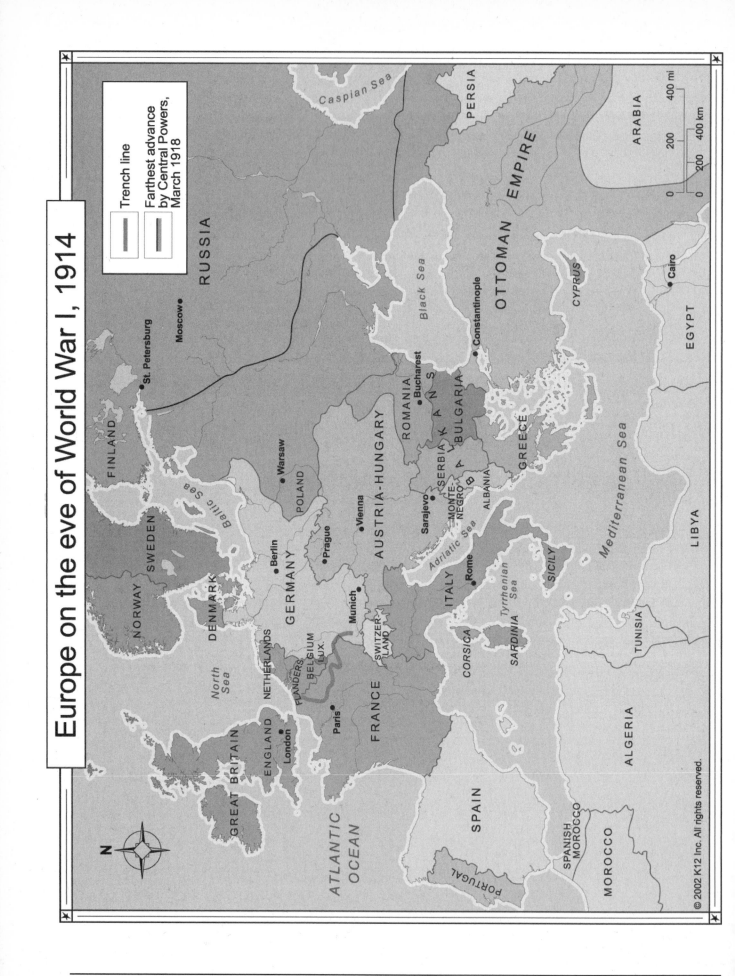

Trench line

Farthest advance by Central Powers, March 1918

RUSSIA

Caspian Sea

PERSIA

ARABIA

OTTOMAN EMPIRE

400 mi

400 km

200

200

0

0

Moscow

St. Petersburg

FINLAND

SWEDEN

NORWAY

Baltic Sea

Warsaw

POLAND

Berlin

Prague

GERMANY

DENMARK

NETHERLANDS

Munich

SWITZER-LAND

BELGIUM

LUX

FLANDERS

Paris

FRANCE

London

ENGLAND

GREAT BRITAIN

North Sea

ATLANTIC OCEAN

SPAIN

PORTUGAL

SPANISH MOROCCO

MOROCCO

ALGERIA

TUNISIA

CORSICA

SARDINIA

Tyrrhenian Sea

ITALY

Rome

SICILY

Mediterranean Sea

LIBYA

AUSTRIA-HUNGARY

Vienna

ROMANIA

Bucharest

Sarajevo

SERBIA

MONTE-NEGRO

ALBANIA

Adriatic Sea

BALKANS

BULGARIA

GREECE

Black Sea

Constantinople

CYPRUS

EGYPT

Cairo

N

Student Guide
Lesson 4: Dashed Hopes

The Great War finally ended at 11 a.m. on November 11, 1918. Woodrow Wilson called it a war to make the world safe for democracy, and a war to end all wars. He asked for a "League of Nations" to stop future wars. But the peace did not live up to his hopes.

Lesson Objectives

- Explain that World War I ended on November 11, 1918, and that that day is remembered as Veterans Day in the U.S.
- Name two terrible results of World War I (such as millions dead; economies ruined; factories, roads, railroads, and buildings destroyed; anger and resentment on all sides).
- Explain that Woodrow Wilson proposed the League of Nations to stop future wars, and that the United States did not join the League.
- Recognize that the peace treaty blamed Germany for the war and demanded reparations.

PREPARE

Approximate lesson time is 60 minutes.

Materials

For the Student

    📖 Map of Europe after World War I, 1920

    📖 Ratifying a Treaty

Keywords and Pronunciation

reparation : Repairs; payment for damages.

LEARN
Activity 1: A War to End All Wars? *(Online)*

To that point, the Great War was the most destructive war in history. Who was to blame? Could Europe be fixed? Who would pay for the destruction? How could a war like this be prevented in the future? As World War I came to a close, these are some of the questions that world leaders had to consider.

Activity 2: History Journal *(Offline)*

It's time to add another chapter to the story of the past. Follow the directions to complete a new entry in your History Journal.

Turn to a new page in your History Journal. On this page, write a paragraph that tells what the lesson was about.

Begin with a topic sentence that introduces the paragraph. Include at least three sentences that give details about the lesson. End with a concluding sentence. You may use the Show You Know questions to help you get started.

When you have finished, check your work. Make sure you have written in complete sentences. Check to make sure you used correct capitalization and punctuation. Date your entry and label it with the lesson title.

Guided Learning: Compare your paragraph with the one in the Teacher Guide.

Activity 3: Ratifying a Treaty *(Offline)*

Print and read the Ratifying a Treaty activity sheet. Then write a short paragraph in your History Journal explaining what a treaty is and how a treaty in the United States is ratified.

ASSESS

Lesson Assessment: Dashed Hopes (*Online*)

You will complete an online assessment covering the main objectives of this lesson. Your assessment will be scored by the computer.

Europe after World War I, 1920

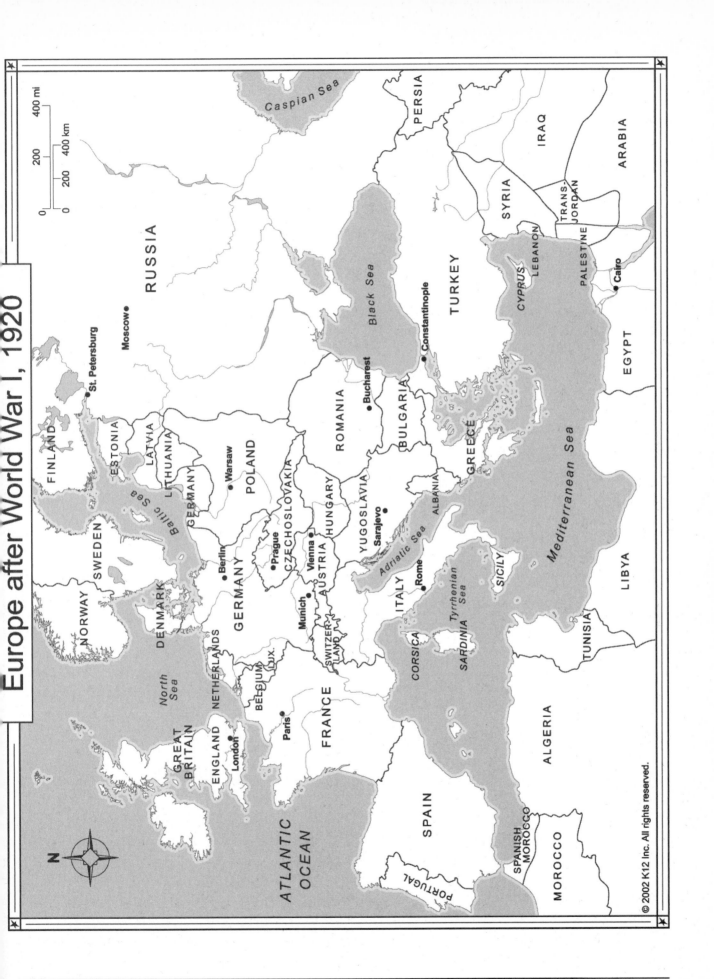

Name _____   Date _____

Ratifying a Treaty

The League of Nations was established by the Treaty of Versailles—the treaty that ended the Great War. Although the League of Nations was President Woodrow Wilson's idea, the United States never joined. Americans were tired of Europe and its wars, and so the U.S. Senate never ratified the Treaty of Versailles.

A **treaty** is an international legal agreement between nations. Treaties are governed by international law.

The U.S. Constitution allows for treaties to be negotiated and agreed to by the Executive Branch—the President.

However, the Constitution also states that a treaty requires the advice and consent of the Senate. This is called *ratification*. Ratification of a treaty requires a two-thirds vote of the Senate.

So . . .

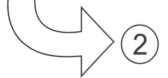

1 President negotiates treaty

2 The Senate approves with a two-thirds vote

Student Guide
Lesson 5: Russia's Czar Dethroned and Lenin Rising

World War I brought much hardship to the Russian people. By the end of the war, they were struggling to survive and weary of the iron rule of the czars. Revolution brought Lenin and his Communist Party to power. Would life for the Russian peasants improve at last?

Lesson Objectives

- Name two hardships suffered by the Russian people in World War I (such as lack of housing; not enough food; not enough fuel to keep warm; many soldiers killed).
- State that revolutionaries overthrew the Russian Czar.
- Describe Lenin as an admirer of Marx's ideas and the founder of the Communist Party in Russia.
- Explain that Lenin ruled Russia as a Communist dictator.

PREPARE

Approximate lesson time is 60 minutes.

Materials

For the Student

📖 Map of Europe after World War I, 1920

Keywords and Pronunciation

Bolsheviks (BOHL-shuh-viks)

dictator (DIK tay tur) : A ruler with absolute power.

soviet : A council.

Vladimir Ilyich Ulyanov (vluh-DYEEM-yir il-YEECH ool-YAH-nef)

LEARN
Activity 1: The Bolsheviks Rule Russia *(Online)*
Read about the changes in Russia from the view of a factory worker.

Activity 2: Report from Russia *(Offline)*
Write a news article in your History Journal about the overthrow of the Russian Czar and the rise to power of the Communist Party.

You were sent to Russia. You talked to a citizen of St. Petersburg. You found out what's going on there. Now your readers want to know what's going on in Russia.

Write a news article about the overthrow of the Russian Czar and the rise to power of the Communist Party. The answers to the following questions will help you get started.

- What were some conditions and factors that helped lead to the Czar being overthrown?
- What kind of government replaced the Czar?
- What political party in Russia believed in the teachings of Karl Marx?
- Who was the leader of that party?
- What did this man, and members of his party, do in October 1917?
- What kind of ruler did this man become?

ASSESS
Lesson Assessment: Russia's Czar Dethroned and Lenin Rising (*Offline*)
You will complete an offline assessment covering the main objectives of this lesson. Your learning coach will score this assessment.

Europe after World War I, 1920

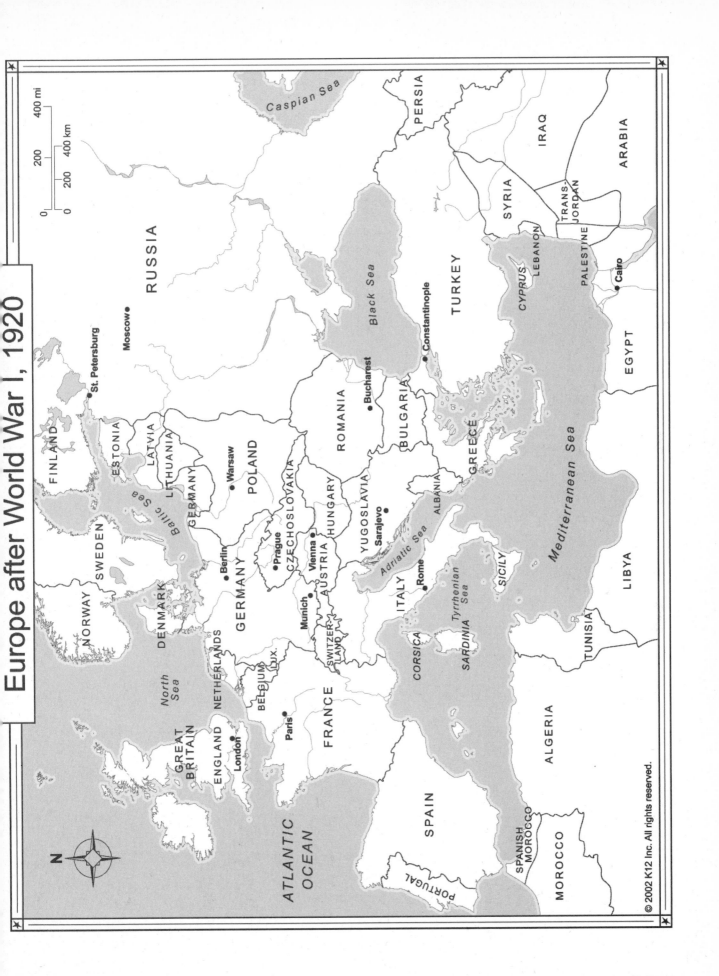

Assessment

History - Unit 9: Mostly Hard Times: World War, 20s, Depression
Lesson 5: In Russia: The Czar Dethroned and Lenin Rising

Name _____ Date _____

In Russia: The Czar Dethroned and Lenin Rising

Fill in the blanks.

1. What were two hardships faced by the Russian people in World War I?

_____

_____

Fill in the blanks using words from the Word Bank below.

2. Revolutionaries in Russia overthrew the Russian _____ .

3. Lenin was an admirer of the ideas of _____ . He founded

   the _____ Party in Russia.

4. _____ ruled Russia as a Communist _____ .

Word Bank

Lenin	king	Marx	Czar	Communist
	president	Republican	dictator	

Student Guide
Lesson 6: From Lenin to Stalin

Russia's Communist Party triumphed in a two-year civil war. It brought several neighboring areas under Communist rule. The new nation was named the Union of Soviet Socialist Republics, or the U.S.S.R. Joseph Stalin succeeded Lenin as a ruthless Communist dictator.

Lesson Objectives

- Explain that after a civil war in Russia, the Communist Party controlled the country.
- Explain that during the war, the Communist army was called the Red Army because of the color of its flag.
- State that after the Communists triumphed, they named their country the Soviet Union, or U.S.S.R.
- Describe Joseph Stalin as a powerful and ruthless dictator who followed Lenin.

PREPARE

Approximate lesson time is 60 minutes.

Materials

For the Student

📖 A Changing Russia

Keywords and Pronunciation

dictator (DIK tay tur) : A ruler with absolute power.

Joseph Stalin (JOH-zuhf STAH-luhn)

Siberia (siy-BIHR-ee-uh)

LEARN
Activity 1: Stalinist Russia (Online)

Activity 2: History Journal (Offline)

It's time to add another chapter to the story of the past. Follow the directions to complete a new entry in your History Journal.

Turn to a new page in your History Journal. On this page, write a paragraph that tells what the lesson was about.

Begin with a topic sentence that introduces the paragraph. Include at least three sentences that give details about the lesson. End with a concluding sentence. You may use the Show You Know questions to help you get started.

When you have finished, check your work. Make sure you have written in complete sentences. Check to make sure you used correct capitalization and punctuation. Date your entry and label it with the lesson title.

Guided Learning: Compare your paragraph with the one in the Teacher Guide.

Activity 3: A Changing Russia *(Offline)*

Print and complete the A Changing Russia activity sheet. Have an adult check your work.

ASSESS

Lesson Assessment: From Lenin to Stalin (*Online*)

You will complete an online assessment covering the main objectives of this lesson. Your assessment will be scored by the computer.

Activity 3: A Changing Russia *(Offline)*

Name _____   Date _____

A Changing Russia

The beginning of the twentieth century was a time of change and turmoil in Russia. It began with a man named Lenin and continued with another named Stalin.

1. Complete the time line below by writing the letter for each event in its correct location.

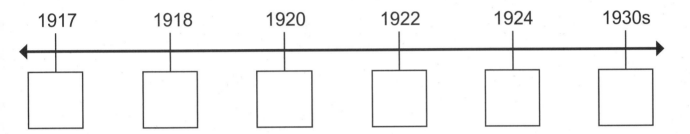

| 1917 | 1918 | 1920 | 1922 | 1924 | 1930s |

A.   A civil war breaks out between the Communists and their enemies.

B.   More than ten million people starve to death on orders of Joseph Stalin.

C.   Lenin and the Communist Party take over most of Russia.

D.   The Red Army defeats the Whites—the civil war is over.

E.   Lenin dies and Joseph Stalin becomes dictator.

F.   Russia is given a new name.

What was Russia's new name?

_____

Because this was such a long name, most people shortened it to

_____

On some maps, you'll even see the initials ___ . ___ . ___ . ___ .

2. During the Russian civil war, the Communist army was called the Red Army. Why?

_____

Color their flag.

3. Describe Stalin's rule. What are some words that describe this man? How was he able to turn the Soviet Union into a major industrial and military power?

_____

_____

_____

_____

_____

_____

Student Guide
Lesson 7: American Women Get the Vote

By the early 1900s more and more people were saying, "Women should be able to vote!" A woman's suffrage movement pressed hard for change. It finally came in 1920, when the 19th Amendment to the American Constitution guaranteed women the right to vote.

Lesson Objectives

- Define *suffrage* as the right to vote.
- Describe the woman's suffrage movement as the movement for the right of women to vote.
- Identify Alice Paul as a leader in the woman's suffrage movement.
- Explain that an amendment to the U.S. Constitution gave women the right to vote.

PREPARE

Approximate lesson time is 60 minutes.

Materials

For the Student
History Journal

Keywords and Pronunciation

picketer : Someone who protests outside a building.

Suffrage : The right to vote.

Suffragist : In this lesson, someone who supports the right of women to vote.

LEARN
Activity 1: A Lady with a Mission *(Online)*

Activity 2: History Journal *(Offline)*

It's time to add another chapter to the story of the past. Follow the directions to complete a new entry in your History Journal.

Turn to a new page in your History Journal. On this page, write a paragraph that tells what the lesson was about.

Begin with a topic sentence that introduces the paragraph. Include at least three sentences that give details about the lesson. End with a concluding sentence. You may use the Show You Know questions to help you get started.

When you have finished, check your work. Make sure you have written in complete sentences. Check to make sure you used correct capitalization and punctuation. Date your entry and label it with the lesson title.

Guided Learning: Compare your paragraph with the one in the Teacher Guide.

Activity 3: Time to Protest (*Offline*)

It's time to protest! Make a sign that could have been carried in the Washington, D.C. suffrage parade. Remember how Alice Paul recruited five thousand women to march in a suffrage parade? They marched in Washington, D.C., the day before Mr. Wilson was sworn in as president. These women carried large signs during their protest march.

Make a sign that could have been carried during this march.

ASSESS

Lesson Assessment: American Women Get the Vote (*Online*)

You will complete an online assessment covering the main objectives of this lesson. Your assessment will be scored by the computer.

Student Guide
Lesson 8: The Roaring '20s

After a terrible world war, Americans shifted their focus away from Europe's problems and toward their own entertainment. The 1920s "roared" with new music and dance. They also roared with a new kind of entertainment--radio and the movies.

Lesson Objectives

- Explain that in the United States, the 1920s was a decade of good times.
- Associate the phrase "Roaring 20s" with the 1920s.
- Name some new forms of entertainment that Americans enjoyed in the 20s, such as jazz, the Charleston, radio.

PREPARE

Approximate lesson time is 60 minutes.

Materials

For the Student

History Journal

📖 Vocabulary of the Roaring 20s

LEARN
Activity 1: A Decade of Good Times *(Online)*

Activity 2: History Journal *(Offline)*

It's time to add another chapter to the story of the past. Follow the directions to complete a new entry in your History Journal.

Turn to a new page in your History Journal. On this page, write a paragraph that tells what the lesson was about. Your work will be used to assess how well you understood the lesson.

Begin with a topic sentence that introduces the paragraph. Include at least three sentences that give details about the lesson. End with a concluding sentence. You may use the Show You Know questions to help you get started.

Include the answers to the following questions in your paragraph:

1. In the United States, what was the decade of the 1920s like?
2. What phrase describes the 1920s?
3. What were some new forms of entertainment that Americans enjoyed in the 20s?

When you have finished, check your work. Make sure you have written in complete sentences. Check to make sure you used correct capitalization and punctuation. Date your entry and label it with the lesson title.

Activity 3: Vocabulary of the Roaring 20s *(Offline)*

The good times of the Roaring Twenties introduced new words and expressions. Print and complete the Vocabulary of the Roaring 20s activity sheet.

Activity 4. Optional: The Roaring '20s *(Offline)*

Learn how to do the Charleston! Step by step directions, accompanied by diagrams, will have you moving to this popular dance from the Roaring 20s. You can even listen to a sample of Charleston music.

ASSESS

Lesson Assessment: The Roaring '20s (*Online*)

Have an adult review your History Journal essay and input the results in the assessment at the end of the lesson.

Name _____ Date _____

Vocabulary of the Roaring 20s

During the good times of the Roaring 20s Americans invented new activities, words, and expressions.

Draw a picture of a flagpole sitter sitting on a flagpole.

Draw a flapper girl.

1. Why did people sit on flagpoles?

_____

_____

_____

2. How did flapper girls wear their hair?

_____

_____

3. What did flapper girls like to do?

_____

_____

_____

4. During the Roaring 20s, families across the country were tuning their radios to a new type of music. This fast and peppy music was called _____.

5. Dancing was another favorite pastime. One very popular dance was the

   _____ .

6. Bees knees was a popular expression in the 20s. Here's how it was used in the story What Would Mama Say!

   - "Look, Howard!" Winnie said. "Doesn't your sister look swell?" Howard turned and grinned. "She's the bee's knees," he said.

   - Life in Chicago was going to be fun! It would be the bee's knees!

   - That decade was "the bee's knees."

   What do you think this expression means?

   _____

   _____

   _____

   _____

Lesson Assessment

The Roaring '20s

Write a paragraph that tells what you have learned. Begin with a topic sentence that introduces the paragraph. Include at least three sentences that give details about what you know. End with a concluding sentence. You may use the Show You Know questions to help you get started.

Include the answers to the following questions in your paragraph:

1. In the United States, what was the decade of the 1920s like?
2. What phrase describes the 1920s?
3. What were some new forms of entertainment that Americans enjoyed in the 20s?

When you have finished, check your work. Make sure you have written in complete sentences. Check to make sure you used correct capitalization and punctuation.

Student Guide
Lesson 9: Charles Lindbergh and Advances in Flight

In his plane, the *Spirit of St. Louis,* Charles Lindbergh was the first person to fly alone across the Atlantic Ocean. His feat inspired millions of people. It also encouraged others to make advances in air travel.

Lesson Objectives

- Describe Charles Lindbergh as the first man to fly solo across the Atlantic Ocean.
- Identify Lindbergh's plane as the *Spirit of St. Louis*.
- Explain that Charles Lindbergh became a hero.
- Explain that Lindbergh used his fame to encourage further work in aviation.

PREPARE

Approximate lesson time is 60 minutes.

Keywords and Pronunciation

aviation : The science of flying; air travel.

LEARN
Activity 1: Lucky Lindy Makes the Hop *(Online)*

Activity 2: History Journal *(Offline)*

It's time to add another chapter to the story of the past. Follow the directions to complete a new entry in your History Journal.

Turn to a new page in your History Journal. On this page, write a paragraph that tells what the lesson was about.

Begin with a topic sentence that introduces the paragraph. Include at least three sentences that give details about the lesson. End with a concluding sentence. You may use the Show You Know questions to help you get started.

When you have finished, check your work. Make sure you have written in complete sentences. Check to make sure you used correct capitalization and punctuation. Date your entry and label it with the lesson title.

Guided Learning: Compare your paragraph with the one in the Teacher Guide.

Activity 3: The Spirit of St. Louis Award (Offline)

Create the Spirit of St. Louis Award for advances in aviation. Print the Student Guide and follow the directions.

After Lindbergh's historic flight across the Atlantic, he worked hard to get people excited about airplanes. In short, Lindbergh used his fame to encourage further work in aviation and rocketry, and he supported experiments with rockets.

Create an award, inspired by Charles Lindbergh, called the Spirit of St. Louis Award. It will be given to one person each year who--like Lindbergh did--helps advance the science of aviation.

This award can be a certificate or a plaque. You could even make a trophy-like award out of clay or some other material. Be creative.

You must also write a short oral presentation that will be read when the award is given--include some information about Lindbergh, his historic flight, and his contributions to aviation and rocketry.

ASSESS

Lesson Assessment: Charles Lindbergh and Advances in Flight (Online)

You will complete an online assessment covering the main objectives of this lesson. Your assessment will be scored by the computer.

LEARN

Activity 4. Optional: Charles Lindbergh and Advances in Flight (Online)

Student Guide
Lesson 10: Fleming and Penicillin: Advances in Medicine

Pasteur had discovered that some bacteria cause diseases. In the 1920s, Alexander Fleming figured out that people could use mold to fight germs! Fleming discovered penicillin, a wonder drug and the first antibiotic.

Lesson Objectives

- Describe antibiotics as drugs that fight harmful bacteria.
- Identify penicillin as the first antibiotic drug.
- Describe penicillin as a powerful antibiotic capable of curing many diseases.
- Identify Alexander Fleming as the British scientist who discovered penicillin.

PREPARE

Approximate lesson time is 60 minutes.

Materials

For the Student

History Journal

📖 The Vocabulary of Antibiotics

Breakthrough: The True Story of Penicillin by Francine Jacobs

Keywords and Pronunciation

antibiotic : A drug made from live microbes that kills harmful bacteria.

bacteria : a kind of microscopic organism.

germs : The common name for disease-causing bacteria.

microbe (MIY-krohb) : A name for any microscopic organism.

Penicillium notatum (pen-ih-SIL-ee-uhm noh-TAH-toum)

Staphylococcus (STA-fuh-loh-KAH-kuhs)

LEARN
Activity 1: Penicillin--The First Antibiotic (Online)

Activity 2: History Journal (Offline)

It's time to add another chapter to the story of the past. Follow the directions to complete a new entry in your History Journal.

Turn to a new page in your History Journal. On this page, copy the following paragraph. Fill in the blanks with words from the Word Bank below. Your work will be used to assess how well you understood the lesson. When you have finished, check your work. Date your entry and label it with the lesson title.

In 1928 a scientist in London made an important discovery. He was looking for a way to kill harmful bacteria. His name was _____. He discovered that a certain mold killed harmful staphylococcus germs. His discovery led to the development of _____, the first antibiotic drug. Antibiotics are _____ that fight harmful _____. Penicillin is a powerful _____ capable of curing many _____.

Word Bank:

Louis Pasteur

Alexander Fleming

penicillin

pasteurization

antibiotic

diseases

drugs

bacteria

Activity 3: The Vocabulary of Antibiotics *(Offline)*

Print and complete The Vocabulary of Antibiotics activity sheet.

ASSESS

Lesson Assessment: Fleming and Penicillin: Advances in Medicine (*Online*)

Have an adult review your History Journal entry and input the results in the assessment at the end of the lesson.

LEARN

Activity 4. Optional: Fleming and Penicillin: Advances in Medicine *(Offline)*

Read *Breakthrough: The True Story of Penicillin* by Francine Jacobs to learn more about the discovery of penicillin. Although Alexander Fleming discovered the mold, many scientists worked to purify and test this miracle drug.

Name _____   Date _____

The Vocabulary of Antibiotics

Write the word for each clue below. Then solve the puzzle at the bottom.

1. A name for any microscopic organism

—— —— —— —— —— —— ——

2. A drug made from live microbes that kills harmful bacteria

—— —— —— —— —— —— —— —— —— ——

3. The first antibiotic drug

—— —— —— —— —— —— —— —— —— ——

4. The mold penicillin is made from

—— —— —— —— —— —— —— —— —— —— ——

—— —— —— —— —— —— ——

5. A deadly germ that can cause deadly infections

—— —— —— —— —— —— —— —— —— —— —— —— ——

6. A kind of microscopic organism

—— —— —— —— —— —— —— ——

7. The common name for disease-causing bacteria

—— —— —— —— ——

8. The man who discovered penicillin: Alexander

__ __ __ __ __ __ __
A   B   C   D   E   F   G

A = The sound that the fourth and fifth letters make together in item 5

B = The seventh letter of item 4

C = The fifth letter of item 6

D = The first letter of item 1

E = The fourth letter of item 2

F = The last letter of item 3

G = The first letter of item 7

Answers: 1. microbe; 2. antibiotic; 3. penicillin; 4. penicillium notatum; 5. Staphylococcus; 6. bacteria; 7. germs; 8. Fleming

Lesson Assessment

Fleming and Penicillin: Advances in Medicine

Fill in the blanks with words from the Word Bank below.

In 1928 a scientist in London made an important discovery. He was looking for a way to kill harmful

bacteria. His name was _____. He discovered that a certain mold killed harmful

staphylococcus germs. His discovery led to the development of _____, the first antibiotic drug.

Antibiotics are _____ that fight harmful _____. Penicillin is a powerful _____

capable of curing many _____.

Word Bank
Louis Pasteur
Alexander Fleming
penicillin
pasteurization
antibiotic
diseases
drugs
bacteria

Student Guide
Lesson 11: The Great Depression

During the Great Depression, thousands of banks, stores, and factories closed. Millions of people were out of work worldwide. In the United States, Franklin Delano Roosevelt had ideas for change. He proved to be the right man for hard times.

Lesson Objectives

- Describe the Great Depression as a time when many banks, stores, and factories closed, and many people lost their jobs.
- Identify Franklin Delano Roosevelt as president of the United States during the Great Depression.
- Explain that Roosevelt started the New Deal, government programs to help get people back to work and give them hope.

PREPARE

Approximate lesson time is 60 minutes.

Keywords and Pronunciation

depression : A time when the economy is very bad; a time when businesses, factories, and stores close, and many people lose their jobs.

Franklin Delano Roosevelt (DEL-uh-noh ROH-zuh-velt)

LEARN
Activity 1: Looking for a Few Good Jobs *(Online)*

Activity 2: History Journal *(Offline)*

It's time to add another chapter to the story of the past. Follow the directions to complete a new entry in your History Journal.

Turn to a new page in your History Journal. On this page, write a paragraph that tells what the lesson was about.

Begin with a topic sentence that introduces the paragraph. Include at least three sentences that give details about the lesson. End with a concluding sentence. You may use the Show You Know questions to help you get started.

When you have finished, check your work. Make sure you have written in complete sentences. Check to make sure you used correct capitalization and punctuation. Date your entry and label it with the lesson title.

Guided Learning: Compare your paragraph with the one in the Teacher Guide.

Activity 3: A Little Research *(Offline)*

Do some research on a topic related to this lesson. Print the Student Guide for directions.

Select one of the following topics to research. (See the Beyond the Lesson activity for some information about the last two topics.)

- Franklin Delano Roosevelt
- the Great Depression
- the New Deal
- Civilian Conservation Corps
- Tennessee Valley Authority

Use nonfiction books, encyclopedias (print or online), and websites as resources for your research.

Select one of the following ways to present information on your topic:

- an oral presentation with visuals
- a written report
- a timeline
- a mobile
- a diorama

ASSESS

Lesson Assessment: The Great Depression (*Offline*)

You will complete an online assessment covering the main objectives of this lesson. Your assessment will be scored by the computer.

LEARN

Activity 4. Optional: The Great Depression *(Online)*

Student Guide
Lesson 12: Unit Review and Assessment

You've completed this unit, and now it's time to review what you've learned and take the unit assessment.

Lesson Objectives

- Demonstrate mastery of important knowledge and skills in this unit.
- Explain that the Great War became a very long and deadly war.
- Name two characteristics of trench warfare on the western front.
- Identify Woodrow Wilson as president of the United States during World War I.
- Recognize that "make the world safe for democracy" was a United States slogan in World War I and a reason for entering the war.
- State that the arrival of U.S. troops in Europe helped the Allies begin to win the war.
- Name two terrible results of World War I (such as millions dead; economies ruined; factories, roads, railroads, and buildings destroyed; anger and resentment on all sides).
- Explain that Woodrow Wilson proposed the League of Nations to stop future wars, and that the United States did not join the League.
- Recognize that the peace treaty blamed Germany for the war and demanded reparations.
- Explain that after a civil war in Russia, the Communist Party controlled the country.
- Describe Joseph Stalin as a powerful and ruthless dictator who followed Lenin.
- Describe the woman's suffrage movement as the movement for the right of women to vote.
- Identify Alice Paul as a leader in the woman's suffrage movement.
- Explain that in the United States, the 1920s was a decade of good times.
- Name some new forms of entertainment that Americans enjoyed in the 20s, such as jazz, the Charleston, radio.
- Describe Charles Lindbergh as the first man to fly solo across the Atlantic Ocean.
- Identify Lindbergh's plane as the *Spirit of St. Louis*.
- Identify penicillin as the first antibiotic drug.
- Identify Alexander Fleming as the British scientist who discovered penicillin.
- Describe the Great Depression as a time when many banks, stores, and factories closed, and many people lost their jobs.
- Identify Franklin Delano Roosevelt as president of the United States during the Great Depression.
- Explain that Roosevelt started the New Deal, government programs to help get people back to work and give them hope.
- Describe Lenin as an admirer of Marx's ideas and the founder of the Communist Party in Russia.

PREPARE

Approximate lesson time is 60 minutes.

LEARN
Activity 1: Mostly Hard Times: War, the Roaring 20s, and Depression (Offline)

We've covered a lot, and now it's time to take a look back. Here's what you should remember about Mostly Hard Times: War, the Roaring 20s, and Depression.

The last twelve lessons have covered just twenty-five years--from 1914 to 1939. That's not much time in history. But those twenty-five years were tough and packed with events!

We began with 1914. Some people say that's when the twentieth century really began. That year the dreadful war that people then called "the Great War" began. What do we call that war today? [1]

World War I fooled everybody. People thought it would be short and glorious. But it wasn't. The war was long and very deadly.

Millions died as nations fought in ways they never had fought before. They used poison gas, tanks, machine guns, and airplanes. On the western front, soldiers dug deep ditches in the ground and just stayed there, firing at each other. What was that kind of warfare called? [2]

What problems did soldiers have with trench warfare? [3]

During World War I, Germany, Austria-Hungary, and the Ottoman Turks lined up on one side. Britain, France, Russia and Italy fought together on the other side.

Americans wanted to stay out of this European war. But when German U-boats sank ships with American civilians aboard, the President said Americans shouldn't stay out any longer. In 1917 the United States entered the war. Who was the American president at the time? [4]

Woodrow Wilson looked at the ambitious Kaiser Wilhelm II, the fierce Ottoman Turks, and the emperor of Austria-Hungary. He said that tyrants like them stood in the way of democracy. He said the United States, the world's greatest republic, would fight to "make the world safe for democracy." That was America's slogan. Everyone also hoped it was going to be "the war to end all wars." It wasn't. But in World War I, American troops and weapons turned the tide. They brought victory to the Allies in 1918.

The peace treaty that ended the war left many nations resentful. One nation was blamed for the war. The treaty said that nation must give up territory and pay huge sums of money to the victors of the war. Which country had to do that? [5]

Many nations did not gain the territory they had expected. Many people did not get their independence. Everyone was unhappy. Still, Woodrow Wilson wanted to make sure such a terrible war would never happen again. He said all nations should be able to talk and sort things out together. What was the name of the international organization he wanted? [6]

It turned out most Americans didn't want to get involved in an international league. They didn't like Wilson's idea. So America never joined the League of Nations.

Meanwhile, in Russia life was dreadful. The Russians had pulled out of World War I before the war ended. They had suffered many deaths and were fed up with Czar Nicholas II. The Russians revolted. What party replaced the czar during the Russian Revolution? [7]

Who was their first important leader? [8]

Lenin turned into a high-handed Communist dictator. He said he would give power to the people. He said that peasants and workers would form councils to govern themselves. What were the workers' councils called? [9]

128

Lenin said "all power to the soviets," but all the power really ended up with Lenin!

Still, Lenin was almost kindly compared to the man who followed him. The new leader's name meant "man of steel," and he certainly was one. Which ruthless dictator followed Lenin? [10]

Stalin renamed Russia the "Union of Soviet Socialist Republics." What was its short name? [11]

Stalin brought farms and industry under state control. He sent millions into slave labor. His policies starved millions more. Meanwhile, he held onto power tightly. The Soviet Union had gotten rid of an almighty czar but it had ended up with an almighty Communist dictator.

There were some bright spots in the 1920s. In the United States and in many nations around the world, women gained a new right. What right did the 19th Amendment to the U.S. Constitution guarantee? [12]

More and more Americans moved from farms to cities. There they enjoyed many new conveniences. Can you name some? [13]

Americans also looked for heroes. One hero flew solo across the Atlantic Ocean. What was his name? [14] Another fellow, a British doctor named Alexander Fleming, was less famous. But he did something that may have been more important. What did Alexander Fleming do? [15] Many people would be saved as a result of Fleming's work.

And during the entire decade the U.S. economy seemed to roar forward. What was this decade called in America? [16]

The "roar" ended with a thud. In 1929 a great world-wide depression descended on America and Europe. Many people lost their jobs. Banks and businesses closed.

In the United States, who was elected president? [17]

Roosevelt used the federal government to start jobs programs. The government built dams, roads, and buildings. Roosevelt's New Deal gave people hope, but even harder times lay ahead. Although Roosevelt said "we have nothing to fear, but fear itself," the world's courage was about to be tested.

Answers

Activity 1

[1] World War I

[2] trench warfare

[3] They could never get dry. There were rats and diseases in the trenches.

[4] Woodrow Wilson

[5] Germany

[6] The League of Nations

[7] the Communist party

[8] Lenin

[9] soviets

[10] Joseph Stalin

[11] the Soviet Union, or the USSR

[12] women's suffrage

[13] radio, refrigerator, electric light, automobiles

[14] Charles Lindbergh

[15] He invented the first antibiotic, penicillin.

[16] the Roaring Twenties

[17] Franklin Delano Roosevelt

Activity 2: Online Interactive Review *(Online)*

ASSESS

Unit Assessment: Mostly Hard Times: War, the Roaring 20s, and Depression
(*Offline*)

Complete an offline Unit Assessment. Your learning coach will score this part of the Assessment.

Name _____ Date _____

Mostly Hard Times

Read each question and its answer choices. Fill in the bubble in front of the word or words that best answer (or complete) the question.

1. Match the name of each person on the left with the correct description on the right.

    E__ Woodrow Wilson

    A. Leader in the women's suffrage movement

    D__ Charles Lindbergh

    B. British scientist who discovered penicillin

    C__ Vladmir Lenin

    C. Founder of the Communist Party in Russia.

    A__ Alice Paul

    D. First person to fly solo across the Atlantic Ocean

    B__ Alexander Fleming

    E. President of the United States during World War I

2. What was World War I called at the time it was being fought?

    (a) The Civil War

    (b) The Final War

    (c) The Great War

    (d) The Trench War

3. Which of the following was an American slogan during World War I—and a reason for entering the war?

   (a) "We have nothing to fear but fear itself!"

   (b) "Take up our quarrel with the foe!"

   (c) "The people need land! The people need bread!"

   (d) "Make the world safe for democracy!"

4. What did the peace treaty that ended World War I say about Germany?

   (a) Germany should take large parts of France and get reparations from England.

   (b) Germany was to blame for the war and should pay reparations.

   (c) Germany should pay back the Ottoman Turks and remove the Kaiser.

   (d) Germany was to keep a large army and police Europe.

5.　Which of the following was NOT true at the end of World War I?

(a)　Millions of people had been killed or wounded.

(b)　There was a lot of anger and resentment in many countries.

(c)　People were hopeful and convinced it was the last war.

(d)　Many factories, roads, and buildings were destroyed.

6.　At the end of World War I, Woodrow Wilson proposed an organization to help nations get together to talk and sort things out. What was it called?

(a)　The League of Nations

(b)　The New Deal Nations

(c)　The Council of Nations

(d)　The Union of Nations

7.　During the Russian Revolution, the people of Russia over-threw their czar. What replaced the czar?

(a)　The Democratic party

(b)　The Communist party

(c)　The Soviet Council

(d)　The Suffragist movement

8. After Lenin, who ruled the Soviet Union as a ruthless dictator?

   ⓐ   Kaiser Wilhelm

   ⓑ   John McCrae

   ⓒ   Nicholas II

   ⓓ   Joseph Stalin

9. In the United States, why were the 1920s known as the Roaring Twenties?

   ⓐ   The country roared with a good economy and good times.

   ⓑ   The country seemed to be roaring toward another world war.

   ⓒ   The country roared along with Franklin Roosevelt's New Deal.

   ⓓ   The country could hear the Great War roaring in Europe.

10. What did women gain from the women's suffrage movement?

   ⓐ   The right to free speech

   ⓑ   The right to protest

   ⓒ   The right to work

   ⓓ   The right to vote

11. Why was the discovery of penicillin important?

(a) Soldiers could drain trenches during World War I.

(b) Countries would have a way to battle the Great Depression.

(c) The world had its first antibiotic drug to fight diseases.

(d) The fighting in World War I could finally come to an end.

12. In 1927, great crowds of people turned out in Paris to meet Charles Lindbergh and

(a) *The Wright Flyer.*

(b) *The Spirit of St. Louis.*

(c) *The Clermont.*

(d) *The Best Friend of Charleston.*

13. Which of the following could you have seen if you had lived in the United States in the 1920s?

(a) Soldiers marching off to the trenches in the Great War

(b) Engineers boarding ships to go build the Panama Canal

(c) Flappers listening to jazz and doing the Charleston

(d) People standing in long lines at telegraph offices

14. The Great Depression was a time when

  (a) many banks and factories closed and people lost their jobs.

  (b) people were sad about what had happened in the Great War.

  (c) World War I ended and many old alliances fell apart.

  (d) people were worried about the diseases caused by bacteria.

15. Which President led the United States during the Great Depression?

  (a) Theodore Roosevelt

  (b) Woodrow Wilson

  (c) Ulysses S. Grant

  (d) Franklin D. Roosevelt

16. What was the "New Deal"?

  (a) A European government program to help people get over the shock of World War I

  (b) A U.S. government program to help people get back to work and give them hope

  (c) A British government program to help people receive all the penicillin they needed

  (d) A Russian government program to help peasants learn about communism

17. Put the following events in chronological order.

  (a) Roaring 20s, Russian Revolution, World War I

  (b) World War I, Great Depression, Roaring 20s

  (c) World War I, Roaring 20s, Great Depression

  (d) Great Depression, World War I, Russian Revolution

18. Essay Question

Write a paragraph about World War I. Start with the topic sentence:
When World War I began, many people thought it would be a short, easy war.

Include the following:
- Tell whether the World War I turned out to be a long, deadly war or a short, easy war.
- Explain what *trench warfare* was, and describe life in the trenches.
- Tell how the arrival of U.S. troops in Europe affected the war.

_____

_____

_____

_____

_____

_____

_____

_____

Student Guide
Lesson 1: The Rise of Dictators

After the horrors of World War I, no one in Europe wanted another war. Yet twenty-one years after the end of the First World War, a Second World War broke out. This second war was greater than any the world had ever seen. More countries fought in it, and more people died in it, than in any other war in history.

The Great Depression affected the whole world. People suffered, and they turned to strong--and often evil-- leaders who promised better times. Nations with no democratic tradition, such as the Soviet Union, Italy, Germany, and Japan, became dictatorships in the 1930s.

Lesson Objectives

- Recognize that in the years after World War I, many nations turned to dictators as leaders.
- Explain that Germany, Italy and Japan attempted to invade and conquer their neighbors.
- Explain that Hitler attempted to conquer large parts of Europe and describe "appeasement" as the Allied response.
- State that Germany, Italy, and Japan fought as the "Axis" powers in World War II, and that Great Britain, the United States, and the Soviet Union fought as the "Allies."
- Define the terms appeasement and blitzkrieg.
- Describe the Holocaust as the Nazi attempt to kill the world's Jews in concentration camps.
- Describe the significance of key events and battles of World War II (Hitler's invasion of Poland, the Battle of Britain, the Holocaust, Pearl Harbor, D-Day, Hiroshima, V-J Day).
- Identify major world leaders during World War II and the countries they led: Hitler, Mussolini, Stalin, Churchill, Franklin Roosevelt, Dwight Eisenhower, Harry Truman.
- Describe the triumph of the Allied powers in World War II as the triumph of democracy over the dictators.
- Explain that World War I left many problems unsolved and the Great Depression affected the whole world.
- Explain that during the Great Depression people were looking for strong leaders who promised order and prosperity.
- Identify Stalin, Hitler, and Mussolini as dictators who led the Soviet Union, Germany, and Italy.
- State that the Japanese were led by a military dictatorship.

PREPARE

Approximate lesson time is 60 minutes.

Materials

For the Student

 📖 Map of Europe on the Eve of World War II

 map, world

 📖 How Could it Happen?

Keywords and Pronunciation

Benito Mussolini (beh-NEE-toh moos-soh-LEE-nee)

dictator (DIK tay tur) : A ruler with absolute power.

LEARN

Activity 1: Strong Leaders Who Promised Much *(Online)*

Print the Europe on the Eve of World War II map and start the lesson.

Activity 2: History Journal *(Offline)*

It's time to add another chapter to the story of the past. Follow the directions to complete a new entry in your History Journal.

Turn to a new page in your History Journal. On this page, write a paragraph that tells what the lesson was about.

Begin with a topic sentence that introduces the paragraph. Include at least three sentences that give details about the lesson. End with a concluding sentence. You may use the Show You Know questions to help you get started.

When you have finished, check your work. Make sure you have written in complete sentences. Check to make sure you used correct capitalization and punctuation. Date your entry and label it with the lesson title.

Guided Learning: Compare your paragraph with the one in the Teacher Guide.

Activity 3: How Could it Happen? *(Offline)*

How could dictators rise to power? Print the How Could it Happen? activity sheet and follow the directions. When you have finished, have an adult check your work.

ASSESS

Lesson Assessment: The Rise of Dictators *(Offline)*

You will complete an offline assessment covering the main objectives of this lesson. Your learning coach will score this assessment.

Europe on the eve of World War II

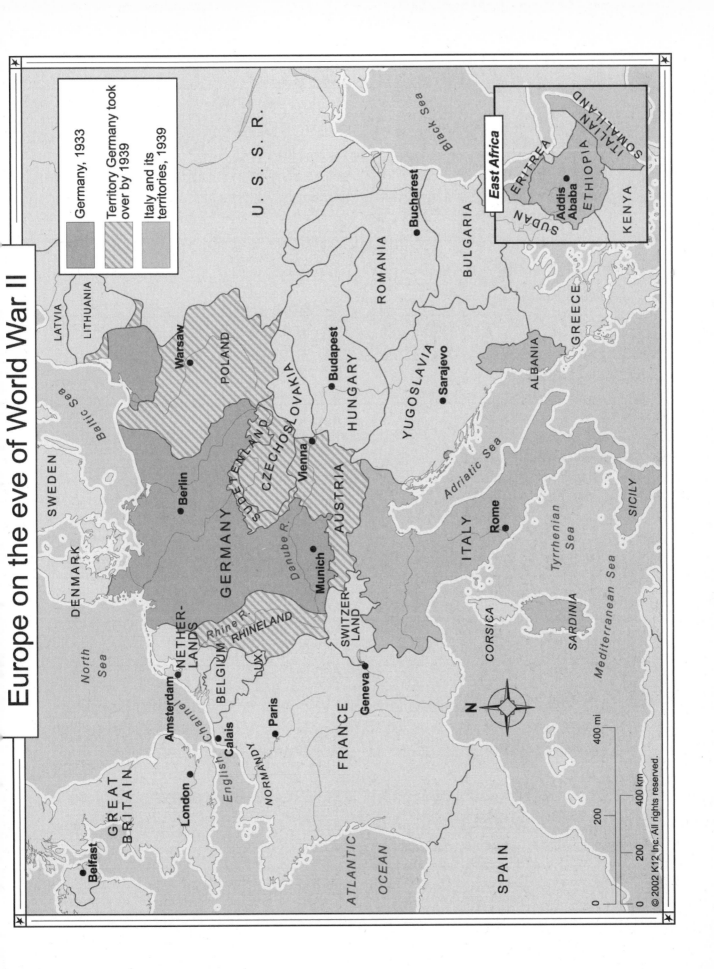

Legend:
- Germany, 1933
- Territory Germany took over by 1939
- Italy and its territories, 1939

GREAT BRITAIN — Belfast, London

North Sea

English Channel — Calais

NORMANDY

FRANCE — Paris, Geneva

SPAIN

ATLANTIC OCEAN

NETHERLANDS — Amsterdam

BELGIUM, LUX.

RHINELAND — Rhine R.

SWITZERLAND

DENMARK

SWEDEN

Baltic Sea

LATVIA

LITHUANIA

U.S.S.R.

POLAND — Warsaw

GERMANY — Berlin, Munich, Danube R.

SUDETENLAND

CZECHOSLOVAKIA

AUSTRIA — Vienna

HUNGARY — Budapest

ROMANIA — Bucharest

Black Sea

BULGARIA

YUGOSLAVIA — Sarajevo

ALBANIA

GREECE

ITALY — Rome

Adriatic Sea

CORSICA

SARDINIA

Tyrrhenian Sea

SICILY

Mediterranean Sea

N

400 mi
400 km
200
200
0
0

East Africa

SUDAN

ERITREA

ITALIAN SOMALILAND

ETHIOPIA — Addis Ababa

KENYA

© 2002 K12 Inc. All rights reserved.

Name _____ Date _____

How Could it Happen?

1. There was trouble in Europe after the Great War. A lot of problems were left unsolved and people were looking for strong leaders.

   Look back at the lesson and find at least three reasons why people were unhappy and angry.

   _____

   _____

   _____

2. These troubled times allowed dictators to rise to power. But life didn't improve with a dictator in control.

   Look back at the lesson and find at least three aspects of life in a dictatorship.

   _____

   _____

   _____

3. One reason dictators were able to rise to power is that they promised to solve problems. People were willing to give these men a chance to fulfill their promises. More often than not, their promises went unfulfilled.

   Look back at the lesson and find at least three promises these dictators made.

   _____

   _____

   _____

How Could it Happen?

4. Would you like living in a country ruled by a dictator? Write two to four sentences explaining why or why not.

_____

_____

_____

_____

_____

Name _____ Date _____

The Rise of Dictators

1. After World War I, problems among nations had been resolved and relations were pretty good.

   (A)   True

   (B)   False

2. The Great Depression only affected the United States.

   (A)   True

   (B)   False

3. During the difficult times after World War I, people were looking for _____ to bring order and prosperity.

   (A)   kings and queens

   (B)   strong leaders

   (C)   new industries

4. What is the word we use to describe rulers such as Stalin, Hitler, and Mussolini who have absolute power? _____

5. Match each leader with the country he led.

   —— Joseph Stalin   A. Italy

   —— Adolph Hitler   B. Soviet Union

   —— Benito Mussolini   C. Germany

6. After World War I, the Japanese were led by —————.

   (A)   monarch

   (B)   military dictators

   (C)   president

Student Guide
Lesson 2: Hitler's Gamble

In the 1930s Japan, Italy, and Germany began to invade other nations. They gambled that the other countries of the world were not ready to fight another war. Hitler posed the biggest threat of all. As the world watched, he invaded one nation after another.

Lesson Objectives

- Explain that Japan, Italy, and Germany began to invade other nations.
- Describe Hitler as the greatest threat to peace and name two areas he conquered.
- Define *appease* and describe *appeasement* as the Allied policy of letting Hitler have what he wanted, hoping it would prolong peace.

PREPARE

Approximate lesson time is 60 minutes.

Materials

For the Student

- 💻 Europe on the Eve of WWII
  History Journal
- 💻 Europe Appeases Hitler
- 💻 Map of Europe on the Eve of World War II

Keywords and Pronunciation

appease : To make peace with someone by giving that person whatever he wants.
Czechoslovakia (cheh-kuh-sloh-VAH-kee-uh)
Sieg heil (zeek hiyl)
Sudetenland (soo-DAY-tun-land)

LEARN
Activity 1: Germany Reaches for Empire (Online)

Activity 2: History Journal (Offline)

It's time to add another chapter to the story of the past. Follow the directions to complete a new entry in your History Journal.

Turn to a new page in your History Journal. On this page, write a paragraph that tells what the lesson was about.

Begin with a topic sentence that introduces the paragraph. Include at least three sentences that give details about the lesson. End with a concluding sentence. You may use the Show You Know questions to help you get started.

When you have finished, check your work. Make sure you have written in complete sentences. Check to make sure you used correct capitalization and punctuation. Date your entry and label it with the lesson title.

Guided Learning: Compare your paragraph with the one in the Teacher Guide.

Activity 3: Europe Appeases Hitler *(Offline)*

Print and complete the Europe Appeases Hitler activity sheet. You'll need the map of Europe on the Eve of World War II to complete the activity. Have an adult check your work. Part of the activity sheet is today's lesson assessment.

ASSESS

Lesson Assessment: Hitler's Gamble (*Offline*)

Have an adult review your answers to the Europe Appeases Hitler activity sheet and input the results online.

Europe on the eve of World War II

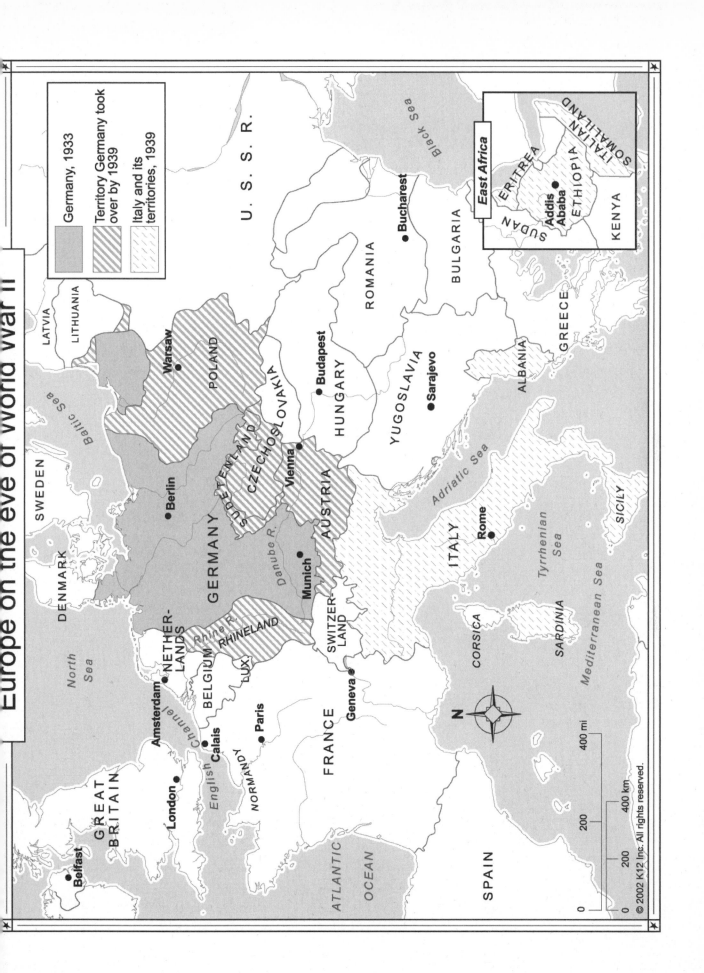

Legend:
- Germany, 1933
- Territory Germany took over by 1939
- Italy and its territories, 1939

GREAT BRITAIN
Belfast
London
Amsterdam
NETHER-LANDS
Calais
NORMANDY
Paris
BELGIUM
LUX.
FRANCE
Geneva
SWITZER-LAND
RHINELAND
Rhine R.
GERMANY
Berlin
Munich
SUDETENLAND
CZECHOSLOVAKIA
Vienna
AUSTRIA
Danube R.
POLAND
Warsaw
LITHUANIA
LATVIA
SWEDEN
DENMARK
North Sea
Baltic Sea
English Channel
ATLANTIC OCEAN
SPAIN
CORSICA
SARDINIA
Tyrrhenian Sea
ITALY
Rome
SICILY
Mediterranean Sea
Adriatic Sea
ALBANIA
GREECE
YUGOSLAVIA
Sarajevo
HUNGARY
Budapest
ROMANIA
Bucharest
BULGARIA
Black Sea
U. S. S. R.

East Africa
SUDAN
ERITREA
ITALIAN SOMALILAND
Addis Ababa
ETHIOPIA
KENYA

N

0   200   400 mi
0   200   400 km

© 2002 K12 Inc. All rights reserved.

Name _____   Date _____

Europe Appeases Hitler

Part 1

Because of the tragedy and devastation of World War I, Europe feared another war. Dictators like Hitler used this to their advantage.

1. On the map of Europe, World War II, color the country that Hitler ruled red.

   European nations like Great Britain and France grew nervous as Germany, Italy, and Japan showed aggressive behavior. To appease Hitler, and avoid war, they let Hitler take the Rhineland, Austria, Czechoslovakia, and the Sudetenland, and the rest of Czechoslovakia.

2. Color Britain and France green on the map.

3. Color the four regions that Hitler invaded light red.

4. What three countries formed the Axis alliance?

   _____   _____   _____

   Locate these three countries on your globe.

Part 2

1. What three countries began to invade other nations in the 1930s?

   _____   _____   _____

2. Which of the dictators of these three countries, posed the greatest threat to peace?

3. Name two nations or regions this dictator conquered.

_____

_____

4. What does the word *appease* mean?

(A) to make war with someone no matter what the risks or costs

(B) to make peace with someone by giving him what he wants

(C) to make alliances with others to protect your own interests

5. Describe the Allied policy of appeasement. In other words, what did the Allies do in response to Hitler's aggression and why?

_____

_____

Europe on the eve of World War II

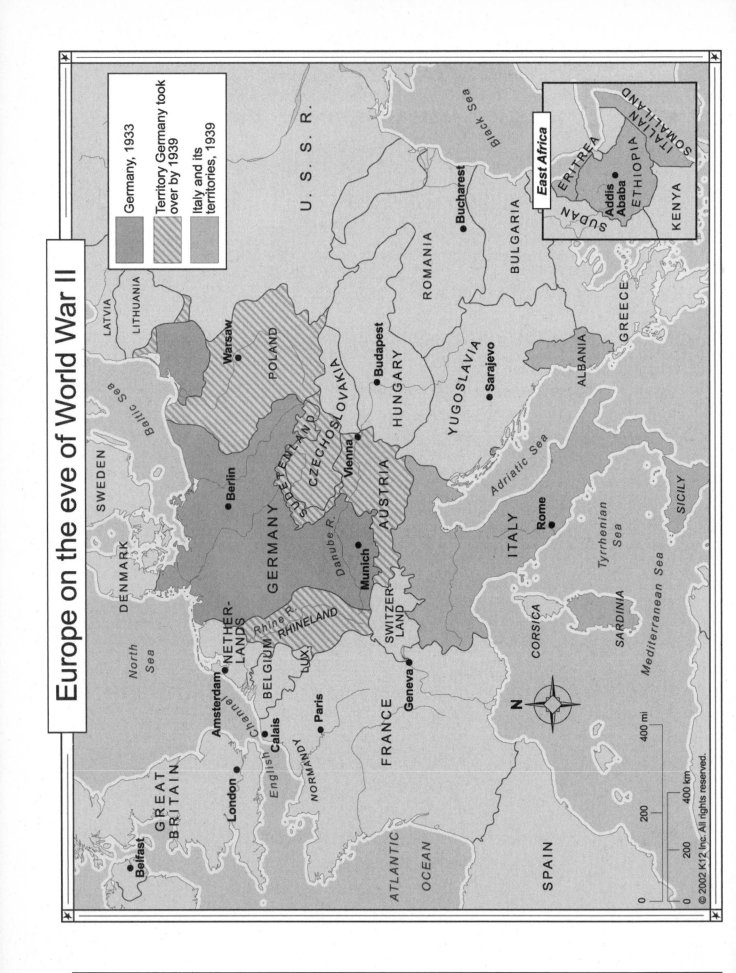

Legend:
- Germany, 1933
- Territory Germany took over by 1939
- Italy and its territories, 1939

GREAT BRITAIN — Belfast, London
NORMANDY, Calais, Paris
FRANCE, Geneva
SPAIN
ATLANTIC OCEAN
English Channel
North Sea
Baltic Sea
SWEDEN
DENMARK
NETHER-LANDS, Amsterdam
BELGIUM, LUX
RHINELAND, Rhine R.
GERMANY, Berlin
SUDETENLAND
SWITZER-LAND
POLAND, Warsaw
CZECHOSLOVAKIA
Danube R.
Munich, Vienna
AUSTRIA
HUNGARY, Budapest
LATVIA
LITHUANIA
U. S. S. R.
ROMANIA, Bucharest
Black Sea
BULGARIA
YUGOSLAVIA, Sarajevo
ALBANIA
GREECE
ITALY, Rome
Adriatic Sea
Tyrrhenian Sea
CORSICA
SARDINIA
SICILY
Mediterranean Sea

East Africa (inset):
SUDAN
ERITREA
ETHIOPIA, Addis Ababa
ITALIAN SOMALILAND
KENYA

N

400 mi
0   200   400
0   200   400 km

© 2002 K12 Inc. All rights reserved.

Lesson Assessment

Hitler's Gamble

1. What three countries began to invade other nations in the 1930s?

    _____   _____   _____

2. Which dictator, of the three countries that began invading other nations in the 1930s, was the greatest threat to his neighbors and to peace? _____

3. Name two nations or regions Hitler conquered.

    _____

    _____

4. What does the word *appease* mean?
    A. to make war with someone no matter what the risks or costs
    B. to make peace with someone by giving him what he wants
    C. to make alliances with others to protect your own interests

5. Describe the Allied policy of appeasement. In other words, what did the Allies do in response to Hitler's aggression and why?

    _____

    _____

Student Guide
Lesson 3: Nazi Blitzkrieg and Axis Expansion

World War II began on September 1, 1939 when Germany invaded Poland. Germany's *blitzkrieg* quickly brought much of Europe under Nazi rule. The Italians battered the British in North Africa. The Japanese, meanwhile, pressed into China and Southeast Asia.

Lesson Objectives
- Explain that when Hitler attacked Poland, Great Britain and France declared war on Germany.
- Explain that the world plunged into a second terrible war called World War II.
- Define *blitzkrieg* as "lightning war" and explain that it was a German attack strategy involving speed and surprise.
- Explain that much of Europe, including France, fell to Hitler during the German *blitzkrieg*.

PREPARE

Approximate lesson time is 60 minutes.

Materials
For the Student

⊡ Hitler's Blitz

⊡ Map of Europe during World War II

History Journal

Keywords and Pronunciation
blitzkrieg (BLITS-kreeg) : A new kind of warfare conducted with great speed and force.

Champs-Élysées (shawn-zay-lee-ZAY)

newsreel : A short movie dealing with current events.

LEARN
Activity 1: Europe Erupts *(Online)*
Print the Europe during World War II map and start the lesson.

Activity 2: History Journal *(Offline)*
It's time to add another chapter to the story of the past. Follow the directions to complete a new entry in your History Journal.

Turn to a new page in your History Journal. On this page, write a paragraph that tells what the lesson was about.

Begin with a topic sentence that introduces the paragraph. Include at least three sentences that give details about the lesson. End with a concluding sentence. You may use the Show You Know questions to help you get started.

When you have finished, check your work. Make sure you have written in complete sentences. Check to make sure you used correct capitalization and punctuation. Date your entry and label it with the lesson title.

Guided Learning: Compare your paragraph with the one in the Teacher Guide.

Activity 3: Hitler's Blitz *(Offline)*

Print and complete the Hitler's Blitz activity sheet. You'll need the map of Europe During World War II, 1940, to complete this activity.

ASSESS

Lesson Assessment: Nazi Blitzkrieg and Axis Expansion (*Online*)

You will complete an online assessment covering the main objectives of this lesson. Your assessment will be scored by the computer.

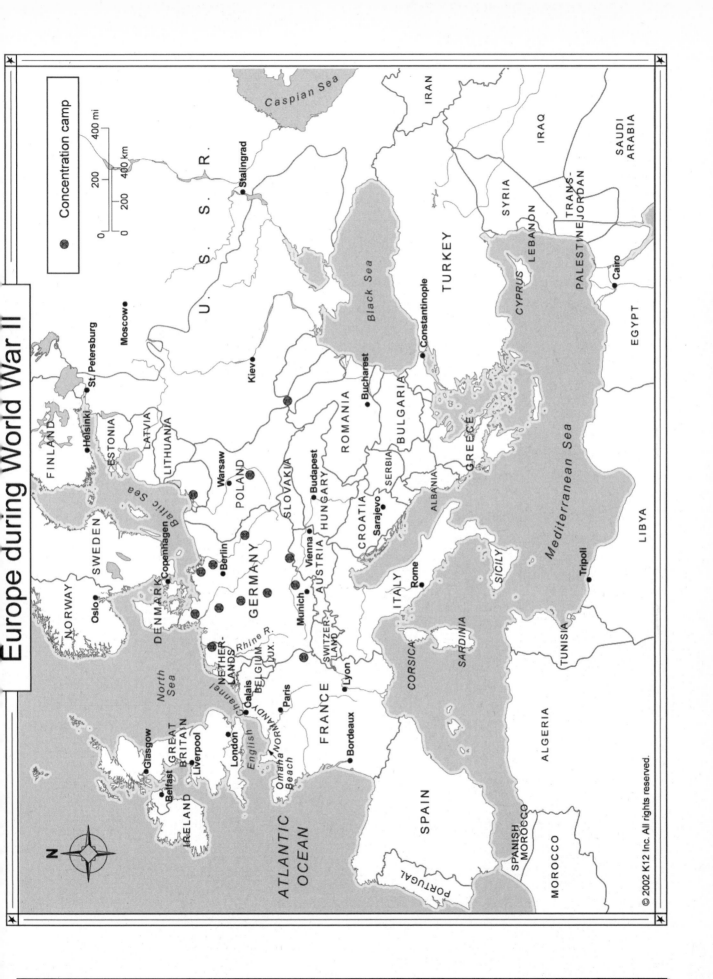

Europe during World War II

Concentration camp

400 mi
400 km

Name _____   Date _____

Hitler's Blitz

Great Britain and France eventually realized that appeasement would not work. Knowing that Hitler had his sights set on Poland, Great Britain and France signed a pact with that country to come to its aid should Germany attack. When German forces raced into Poland in September, 1939, Europe plunged into war.

1. On the map of Europe (During World War II, 1940), write a "1" in Poland and color that country light red.

   Using a new style of warfare called a *blitzkrieg*, the German army invaded Denmark and Norway.

2. Write a "2" in Denmark and Norway and color them light red.

   Then Hitler moved west. He swept into Belgium, Holland, and Luxembourg, using dive bombers to terrify civilians.

3. Write a "3" in Belgium, Holland, and Luxembourg and color these countries light red.

   Hitler then eyed France. Though many thought France would hold out against the Nazis, it soon fell to the German's lightning quick attacks. Most of Europe had fallen under the Nazi dictatorship of Adolph Hitler.

4. Write a "4" in France and color it light red.

   The eyes of the world would turn toward Britain. Many wondered if the British would stand alone or become the next victim of Hitler's lightning war.

5. Color Great Britain green.

6. The terrible war that Europe was plunged into is called

   _____ .

7. What does the German word *blitzkrieg* mean?

   _____

Student Guide
Lesson 4: Churchill Leads Embattled Britain

After France surrendered, Hitler planned to invade England. The Germans began to bomb London in preparation. But Hitler hadn't counted on Winston Churchill, the Royal Air Force, and British resolve.

Lesson Objectives

- Identify Winston Churchill as the prime minister of Great Britain during World War II.
- Explain that in the Battle of Britain, the Nazis launched air attacks on London and were defeated by the Royal Air Force.
- Explain that Churchill led Great Britain through the Battle of Britain.
- State that Hitler invaded the Soviet Union, widening the war to the east.

PREPARE

Approximate lesson time is 60 minutes.

LEARN
Activity 1: Britain Stands Alone (Online)

Activity 2: Letter for Help (Offline)

Every Londoner knew the battle was coming. Now German bombers were beginning to fill the skies. Write a letter to relatives in the country asking if your children can stay with them during this hard time.

When the air raids started, families living in London began sending their children to safety in the countryside. Imagine you're living in London. The Battle of Britain has started. Write a letter to a relative who lives in the country.

In your letter:

- Explain the current situation in London.
- Describe the danger Hitler poses to England.
- Mention who is leading the country through the Battle of Britain.
- Ask if you can send your children to them so the children will be safe.

Guided Learning: Have an adult check your work, and then place it in your History Journal.

ASSESS

Lesson Assessment: Churchill Leads Embattled Britain (*Online*)

You will complete an online assessment covering the main objectives of this lesson. Your assessment will be scored by the computer.

Student Guide
Lesson 5: The Holocaust

Hitler blamed Germany's problems on the Jews, and he wanted them dead. The mass murder of millions of Jews by the Nazis is called the Holocaust. The story of Anne Frank shows us the courage and hope of a Jewish family and their neighbors during hard times.

Lesson Objectives

- Explain that Hitler blamed Germany's problems on the Jews.
- Describe the Holocaust as the mass murder of millions of Jews by the Nazis.
- Explain that concentration camps were places where many Jews were taken, tortured and killed.
- Explain that Anne Frank was a Jewish girl who hid with her family.

PREPARE

Approximate lesson time is 60 minutes.

Materials

For the Student

History Journal

🖥 Anne Frank activity sheet

Keywords and Pronunciation

Holocaust : The mass murder of millions of Jews in World War II.

LEARN
Activity 1: Anne Frank's Story (Online)

Activity 2: History Journal (Offline)

It's time to add another chapter to the story of the past. Follow the directions to complete a new entry in your History Journal.

Turn to a new page in your History Journal. On this page, write a paragraph that tells what the lesson was about.

Begin with a topic sentence that introduces the paragraph. Include at least three sentences that give details about the lesson. End with a concluding sentence. You may use the Show You Know questions to help you get started.

When you have finished, check your work. Make sure you have written in complete sentences. Check to make sure you used correct capitalization and punctuation. Date your entry and label it with the lesson title.

Guided Learning: Compare your paragraph with the one in the Teacher Guide.

Activity 3: Anne Frank *(Offline)*

Print and complete the Anne Frank activity sheet.

ASSESS

Lesson Assessment: The Holocaust *(Online)*

You will complete an online assessment covering the main objectives of this lesson. Your assessment will be scored by the computer.

LEARN

Activity 4. Optional: The Holocaust *(Online)*

Learn more about Anne Frank at Anne Frank Online.

Name_____   Date_____

Anne Frank

The Great Depression affected many nations around the world, including Germany. And in Germany, people were still angry about how they had been treated by the victors after World War I.

1. Who did Hitler and the Nazis blame for Germany's problems?_____

The Nazis decided to solve the problem of the Jews by sending them to concentration camps.

2. What were concentration camps? _____

_____

Many Jews left Germany and fled to other countries, such as the Netherlands and France. But when Germany invaded those countries, the Jews were once more in danger.

3. What was the mass murder of millions of Jews by the Nazis called?

_____

Many Jewish families tried to escape the concentration camps by hiding from the Nazis.

4. Who was a Jewish girl who hid with her family from the Nazis?

_____

"It's a wonder I haven't abandoned all my ideals, they seem so absurd and impractical. Yet I cling to them because I still believe, in spite of everything, that people are truly good at heart."

From Anne Frank's diary, July 15, 1944

Student Guide
Lesson 6: Pearl Harbor and United States Entry into the War

Americans were reluctant to enter World War II. Then, on December 7, 1941, Japan launched a surprise attack on the U.S. navy base at Pearl Harbor. President Franklin Roosevelt called it "a date which will live in infamy." The United States declared war on the Axis powers.

Lesson Objectives

- Explain that the Japanese launched a surprise attack on the U.S. Naval Base at Pearl Harbor in Hawaii on December 7, 1941.
- Recognize the phrase "a date which will live in infamy" as the words President Roosevelt used to describe the attack on Pearl Harbor.
- Explain that the attack on Pearl Harbor brought the United States into World War II.

PREPARE

Approximate lesson time is 60 minutes.

Materials

>   For the Student
>
>   map, world
>
>   History Journal
>
>   🖳 A Date Which Will Live in Infamy activity sheet

Keywords and Pronunciation

infamy : A reputation for evil.

LEARN
Activity 1: Japan's Expanding Empire *(Online)*

Activity 2: History Journal *(Offline)*

It's time to add another chapter to the story of the past. Follow the directions to complete a new entry in your History Journal.

Turn to a new page in your History Journal. On this page, write a paragraph that tells what the lesson was about.

Begin with a topic sentence that introduces the paragraph. Include at least three sentences that give details about the lesson. End with a concluding sentence. You may use the Show You Know questions to help you get started.

When you have finished, check your work. Make sure you have written in complete sentences. Check to make sure you used correct capitalization and punctuation. Date your entry and label it with the lesson title.

Guided Learning: Compare your paragraph with the one in the Teacher Guide.

Activity 3: A Date Which Will Live in Infamy *(Offline)*
Print and complete the A Date Which Will Live in Infamy activity sheet.

ASSESS
Lesson Assessment: Pearl Harbor and United States Entry into the War
(Online)
You will complete an online assessment covering the main objectives of this lesson. Your assessment will be scored by the computer.

LEARN
Activity 4. Optional: Pearl Harbor and United States Entry into the War *(Online)*
Learn more about the attack on Pearl Harbor at this National Geographic website.

Name _____ Date _____

A Date Which Will Live in Infamy

The following is part of the speech Franklin Roosevelt gave to Congress the day after the attack on Pearl Harbor. Read this excerpt and then answer the questions that follow.

Yesterday, December 7, 1941—a date which will live in infamy—the United States of America was suddenly and deliberately attacked by naval and air forces of the Empire of Japan.

The United States was at peace with that nation and, at the solicitation of Japan, was still in conversation with its government and its emperor looking toward the maintenance of peace in the Pacific.

Indeed, one hour after Japanese air squadrons had commenced bombing in Oahu, the Japanese ambassador to the United States and his colleagues delivered to the secretary of state a formal reply to a recent American message. While this reply stated that it seemed useless to continue the existing diplomatic negotiations, it contained no threat or hint of war or armed attack.

It will be recorded that the distance of Hawaii from Japan makes it obvious that the attack was deliberately planned many days or even weeks ago. During the intervening time the Japanese government has deliberately sought to deceive the United States by false statements and expressions of hope for continued peace.

1. What were relations between the United States and Japan like before the attack?

_____

2. Did Japan give any hints or threats that an attack was about to come?

_____

3. When the Japanese ambassador to the United States delivered the message "that it seemed useless to continue the existing diplomatic negotiations," had Japan already made plans to attack Pearl Harbor?

_____

4. Based on this excerpt from Roosevelt's speech, why do you think Americans were so surprised and angered by Japan's attack on Pearl Harbor?

_____

_____

Student Guide
Lesson 7: D-Day and Victory in Europe

Hitler's forces had rolled across much of Europe, but the Allies fought back. With the United States in the war, the Allies launched an invasion of Europe. D-Day, led by General Dwight D. Eisenhower, turned the tide of the war.

Lesson Objectives

- Explain that D-Day was the day of a huge Allied invasion of France from across the English Channel.
- Name Dwight D. Eisenhower as the commander of the Allied invasion force.
- Recognize that the Allies suffered great losses on D-Day, but that the invasion turned the tide of the war.
- State that Germany surrendered to the Allies in 1945.

PREPARE

Approximate lesson time is 60 minutes.

Materials

> For the Student
>> 🖥 Map of Europe during World War II
>> History Journal
>> 🖥 From England to Berlin

Keywords and Pronunciation

Bergen-Belsen (BEHR-guhn-BEL-zuhn)
Buchenwald (BOO-kuhn-vahlt)
Calais (ka-LAY)
Champs-Élysées (shawn-zay-lee-ZAY)
Dwight D. Eisenhower (dwiyt dee IYZ-uhn-how-ur)

LEARN
Activity 1: Invading Nazi Europe *(Online)*

Activity 2: History Journal *(Offline)*

It's time to add another chapter to the story of the past. Follow the directions to complete a new entry in your History Journal.

Turn to a new page in your History Journal. On this page, write a paragraph that tells what the lesson was about.

Begin with a topic sentence that introduces the paragraph. Include at least three sentences that give details about the lesson. End with a concluding sentence. You may use the Show You Know questions to help you get started.

When you have finished, check your work. Make sure you have written in complete sentences. Check to make sure you used correct capitalization and punctuation. Date your entry and label it with the lesson title.

Guided Learning: Compare your paragraph with the one in the Teacher Guide.

Activity 3: From England to Berlin (Offline)

Print and complete the From England to Berlin activity sheet. You'll need the map from the lesson to complete this activity.

ASSESS

Lesson Assessment: D-Day and Victory in Europe (Online)

You will complete an online assessment covering the main objectives of this lesson. Your assessment will be scored by the computer.

LEARN

Activity 4. Optional: D-Day and Victory in Europe (Online)

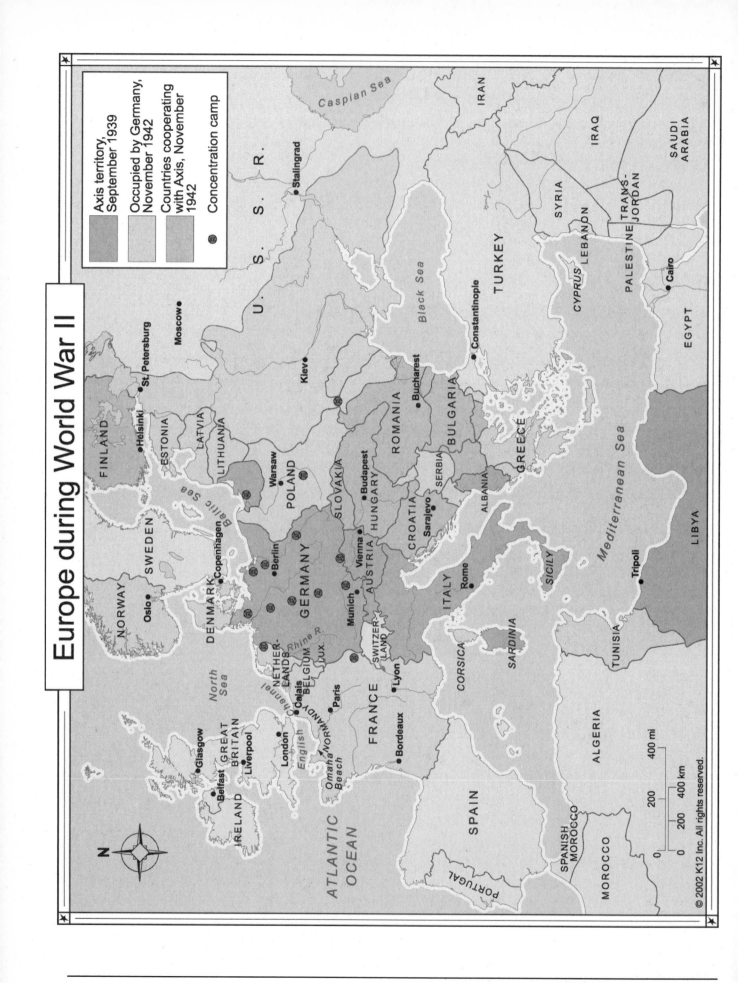

Europe during World War II

Legend:
- Axis territory, September 1939
- Occupied by Germany, November 1942
- Countries cooperating with Axis, November 1942
- ● Concentration camp

Bodies of water and regions:
Caspian Sea, Black Sea, Baltic Sea, North Sea, Mediterranean Sea, ATLANTIC OCEAN, English Channel, Rhine R.

Countries/regions:
IRAN, IRAQ, SAUDI ARABIA, SYRIA, LEBANON, CYPRUS, PALESTINE, TRANS-JORDAN, EGYPT, TURKEY, GREECE, ALBANIA, BULGARIA, SERBIA, ROMANIA, CROATIA, HUNGARY, AUSTRIA, SLOVAKIA, POLAND, U. S. S. R., FINLAND, SWEDEN, NORWAY, ESTONIA, LATVIA, LITHUANIA, DENMARK, GERMANY, NETHER-LANDS, BELGIUM, LUX., SWITZER-LAND, FRANCE, ITALY, SICILY, SARDINIA, CORSICA, SPAIN, PORTUGAL, MOROCCO, SPANISH MOROCCO, ALGERIA, TUNISIA, LIBYA, GREAT BRITAIN, IRELAND, NORMANDY

Cities:
Stalingrad, Moscow, St. Petersburg, Helsinki, Kiev, Constantinople, Bucharest, Cairo, Warsaw, Budapest, Berlin, Copenhagen, Vienna, Sarajevo, Rome, Munich, Oslo, Tripoli, Lyon, Paris, Calais, London, Liverpool, Belfast, Glasgow, Bordeaux, Omaha Beach

Scale:
400 mi
0 200 400 km

N

Name _____   Date _____

From England to Berlin

With most of Europe under Hitler's control, the Allies (United States, England, and the Soviet Union) agreed to work together to defeat Nazi Germany.

1. On the map of Europe during World War II, lightly shade Axis territory as of September 1939.

2. In a different color, shade territory occupied by Germany by November 1942.

3. In a different color, shade those countries that were cooperating with the Axis powers in November 1942.

While the Soviets continued fighting Germans in the east, the British and Americans made plans to invade France from across the English Channel.

4. What do we call the day of this huge Allied invasion of France?

_____

Although many worked hard, and in secret, to plan the invasion, leadership of the invasion force fell to one man.

5. Who was the commander of the Allied invasion force? _____

6. On the map, draw an arrow from England to Normandy. Color the English Channel blue.

Although the Allies suffered great losses at Normandy, the invasion was a success. Allied forces had gained a foothold on the continent and began to roll through France. The German army retreated before the advancing Allied forces. Soon, American and British soldiers were liberating Paris.

7. Draw an arrow from the beaches of Normandy to Paris.

From England to Berlin

Meanwhile, the Soviets were advancing along the eastern front, pushing the Germans back.

8. Draw an arrow from Moscow, pointing toward Berlin.

As Allied troops fought their way eastward toward Berlin, they liberated many concentration camps.

9. What were the two concentration camps that were liberated by Allied troops?

_____

Finally the war closed in on the German capital of Berlin, as Allied forces entered the city from the west and the east. Knowing the war was over, Hitler committed suicide. A week later the Germans surrendered.

10. What was the month and year? _____

Student Guide
Lesson 8: The Atomic Bomb and V-J Day

After the United States dropped the atomic bomb on the Japanese cities of Hiroshima and Nagasaki, Japan surrendered. World War II came to an end. But the atomic age had begun.

Lesson Objectives

- Describe the atomic bomb as an incredibly powerful bomb developed secretly in the United States during World War II.
- Explain that the United States used the atomic bomb on Hiroshima and Nagasaki to end the war.
- Name some of the effects of the bomb, such as whole cities destroyed, many people killed, sickness from radiation.
- State that the Japanese surrendered shortly after the bombing of Nagasaki.

PREPARE

Approximate lesson time is 60 minutes.

Materials

For the Student

    📖 Map of Pacific Theater, 1945

    History Journal

    📖 War in the Pacific Ends

Keywords and Pronunciation

Hiroshima (hee-roh-SHEE-mah)

Nagasaki (nah-gah-SAH-kee)

uranium (yoo-RAY-nee-uhm)

LEARN
Activity 1: Victory in the Pacific (Online)
Print the Pacific Theater, 1945 map and start the lesson.

Activity 2: History Journal (Offline)
It's time to add another chapter to the story of the past. Follow the directions to complete a new entry in your History Journal.

Turn to a new page in your History Journal. On this page, write a paragraph that tells what the lesson was about.

Begin with a topic sentence that introduces the paragraph. Include at least three sentences that give details about the lesson. End with a concluding sentence. You may use the Show You Know questions to help you get started.

When you have finished, check your work. Make sure you have written in complete sentences. Check to make sure you used correct capitalization and punctuation. Date your entry and label it with the lesson title.

Guided Learning: Compare your paragraph with the one in the Teacher Guide.

Activity 3: War in the Pacific Ends *(Offline)*

Print and complete the War in the Pacific Ends activity sheet. Have an adult check your work.

ASSESS

Lesson Assessment: The Atomic Bomb and V-J Day (*Online*)

You will complete an online assessment covering the main objectives of this lesson. Your assessment will be scored by the computer.

Pacific Theater, 1945

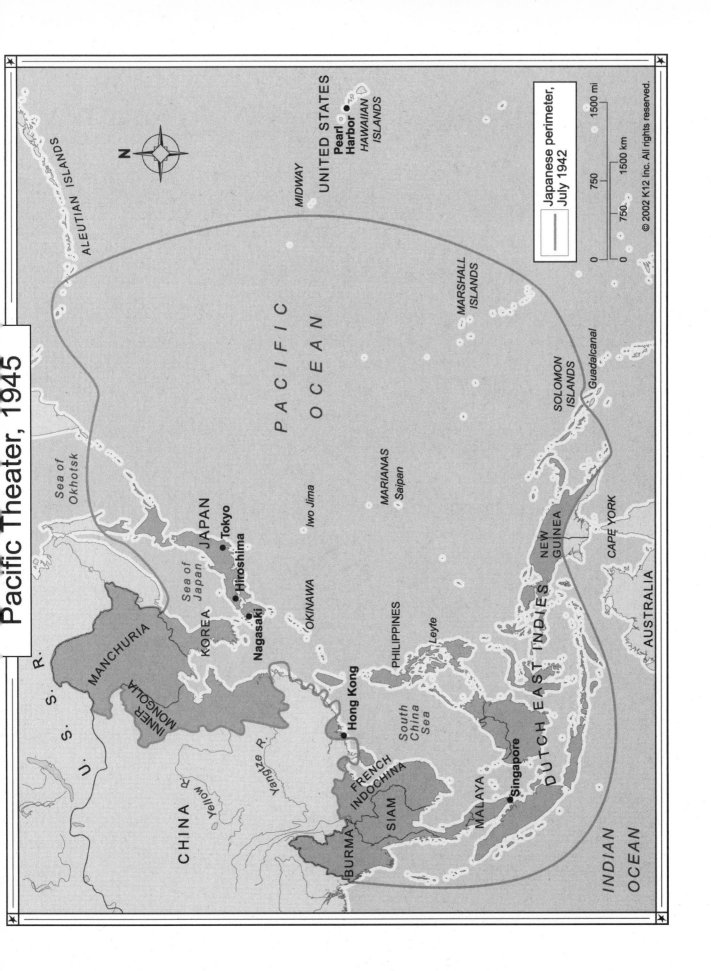

Name _____ Date _____

War in the Pacific Ends

Japan had enlarged its empire in the Pacific by conquering countries such as Burma, Malaya, the Dutch East Indies, Singapore, and the Philippines. In addition, Japanese forces had invaded smaller islands throughout the Pacific. But the tide of war began to turn against Japan. American troops, along with allied troops from Australia and New Zealand, began island hopping across the Pacific, retaking islands that had fallen to the Japanese.

1. The first major victory comes at the Battle of Midway, June 3-6, 1942. Circle the Midway Islands on the map of the Pacific Theater, 1945, and label it "1."

2. On August 7 of the same year, Americans land on Guadalcanal, in the Solomon Islands. Circle the Solomon Islands and label them "2."

3. Allied forces continue making progress and land on Saipan, in the Marianas Islands, on June 15, 1944. Circle the Marianas Islands and label them "3."

4. There was much fierce fighting in the jungles of the Philippines. On October 20, 1944, American troops land on Leyte Island in the Philippines. Circle the Philippine Islands and label them "4."

5. The Allied forces continue moving northward, toward Japan. On February 19, 1945, the amphibious assault of Iwo Jima begins. Circle and label that island "5." Less than two months later, the Allied invasion of Okinawa begins. Circle and label Okinawa "6."

War in the Pacific Ends

Although the Allies were winning the war and Tokyo lay in ruins, Japan showed no sign of giving up. It looked like the Allies would have to launch a huge invasion of Japan. But President Truman had another option – the atomic bomb.

6. The atomic bomb was a very _____ bomb. It was developed

   secretly by the United States during _____ .

7. To end the war, the United States dropped atomic bombs on the cities of Hiroshima and Nagasaki. Circle these two cities on the map.

8. The effects of the bombs were terrible. Describe at least two of the effects.

   _____

   _____

9. Despite the tragic effects of using the atomic bomb, it's believed that, in the

   end, thousands of lives were saved. The reason is that shortly after the

   bombs were dropped, Japan _____ . World War II was finally over.

Student Guide
Lesson 9: Unit Review and Assessment

You've completed this unit, and now it's time to review what you've learned and take the unit assessment.

Lesson Objectives

- Demonstrate mastery of important knowledge and skills in this unit.
- Identify Winston Churchill as the prime minister of Great Britain during World War II.
- Identify Stalin, Hitler, and Mussolini as dictators who led the Soviet Union, Germany, and Italy.
- Define *appease* and describe *appeasement* as the Allied policy of letting Hitler have what he wanted, hoping it would prolong peace.
- Explain that when Hitler attacked Poland, Great Britain and France declared war on Germany.
- Define *blitzkrieg* as "lightning war" and explain that it was a German attack strategy involving speed and surprise.
- Explain that in the Battle of Britain, the Nazis launched air attacks on London and were defeated by the Royal Air Force.
- Describe the Holocaust as the mass murder of millions of Jews by the Nazis.
- Explain that Anne Frank was a Jewish girl who hid with her family.
- Explain that the Japanese launched a surprise attack on the U.S. Naval Base at Pearl Harbor in Hawaii on December 7, 1941.
- Recognize the phrase "a date which will live in infamy" as the words President Roosevelt used to describe the attack on Pearl Harbor.
- Explain that the attack on Pearl Harbor brought the United States into World War II.
- Explain that D-Day was the day of a huge Allied invasion of France from across the English Channel.
- Name Dwight D. Eisenhower as the commander of the Allied invasion force.
- Explain that the United States used the atomic bomb on Hiroshima and Nagasaki to end the war.
- State that the Japanese surrendered shortly after the bombing of Nagasaki.
- Recognize that in the years after World War I, many nations turned to dictators as leaders.
- State that Germany, Italy, and Japan fought as the "Axis" powers in World War II, and that Great Britain, the United States, and the Soviet Union fought as the "Allies."

PREPARE

Approximate lesson time is 60 minutes.

LEARN
Activity 1: World War II *(Offline)*

We've covered a lot, and now it's time to take a look back. Here's what you should remember about World War II.

After the horrors of World War I, no one in Europe wanted another war. Yet twenty-one years after the end of the First World War, a Second World War broke out. This second war was greater than any the world had ever seen. More countries fought in it, and more people died in it, than any war in history.

How did it happen? Why did the countries of the world fight each other for six long years? Why did they ruin cities, destroy whole economies, and kill millions of soldiers and civilians? Let's think back.

We've said that World War II was a war that no one wanted. Well, almost no one wanted it. At least one man was ready to fight. If he didn't get his way, he was ready to plunge the world into war. He was the leader of Germany, and he became its dictator. What was his name? [1]

Adolf Hitler fired up the German people. Germany had lost World War I, and Germans were angry. Hitler told them that Germans should be angry. He said they were a superior people, a master race!

Hitler blamed everyone else for Germany's problems. He blamed the victors in World War I. He blamed the Jews. He told Germans their country would be powerful again. Nations that stood in their way would be crushed. Jews would be crushed.

"Nationalism" sometimes means believing your country is better than anyone else's. Hitler was a nationalist. His party took its name from the German word for "nationalist." What was the name of his political party? [2]

Hitler and the Nazis decided they would take what they wanted. If anyone objected, Hitler threatened war. Now, Hitler was just one of the dictators in power in the 1930s. Italy had a dictator, too. Do you remember his name? [3]

The island nation of Japan had set up a military dictatorship as well.

Hitler had watched these other dictatorships with interest. He had seen how the Italians conquered territory in Africa. He had seen how the Japanese invaded countries in Asia. And he had seen how the democracies of the world had done nothing to stop them. Hitler grew bold. He began to make his own grab for territory.

Democratic nations such as Britain and France were terrified at the thought of another war. When Hitler began to take over territories, Britain and France tried to appease him. What does appease mean? [4]

Britain and France hoped they could keep the peace by giving Hitler what he wanted. But Hitler never seemed to get enough! After he got one territory, he demanded another. And another. He marched an army into the Rhineland. He took over Austria. He grabbed Czechoslovakia.

Finally, Britain and France could appease Hitler no more. When the German dictator invaded Poland, they declared war. World War II began.

Like a streak of lightning, German armies flashed across Europe. Country after country fell. The Germans struck with speed and surprise. There is a special name for this kind of warfare. Do you remember what it is called? [5]

France was one of the countries that Germany conquered. Soon Britain stood alone. German airplanes pounded the island during the Battle of Britain. But the British held out. They refused to surrender. Who was the prime minister who led Great Britain during this country's darkest hour? [6]

Hitler failed to defeat Britain. So he wheeled his armies east and invaded another country. This country was led by the communist dictator, Joseph Stalin. What country was it? [7]

The Second World War was expanding. On December 7, 1941, it expanded more. On that "date that will live in infamy," Japan attacked the United States. Where did the Japanese strike? [8]

Which president led America into World War II? [9]

The two sides in the war were known as the Allied powers and the Axis powers. There were four Allies. Name three of them. [10]

Name the three Axis powers. [11]

The Allies fought the Axis powers all over the world. The Allies launched a bold invasion of Europe from Britain. It was led by an American general named Dwight Eisenhower. Do you remember what the day of the invasion was called? [12]

The Allies pressed east and pushed the German army back into Germany. As they pushed forward, they saw for themselves one of the greatest horrors of World War II. Hitler had been trying to kill all of the world's Jews in concentration camps. Allied troops couldn't believe their eyes and quickly liberated survivors. What was this terrible mass murder of Jews called? [13]

The war was now nearing its end. U.S. and British troops were closing in on Germany from the west. Soviet forces were advancing from the east. Germany surrendered.

In Asia the Japanese were still fighting. They battled fiercely for every inch of territory. By now the United States had a new president. What was his name? [14]

Harry Truman knew that millions might die in Asia before the fighting ended. Allied scientists had developed a new kind of weapon. It was a weapon of incredible power that could cause great destruction. Do you remember what it was called? [15]

Truman decided to use the atomic bomb. American planes dropped atomic bombs on two Japanese cities. Can you name them? [16]

The Japanese surrendered. That day was known as V-J Day--Victory in Japan Day.

Hitler, Mussolini, and the Japanese military had been stopped. The world would be a better place. The dictators were not just enemies of freedom and peace; they were butchers. Their goal was to gain power for themselves and destroy everyone standing in their way. They didn't want anyone else to have rights. In the end, though, the world's great democracies defeated them. The world was at peace. The challenge would be to rebuild a better world.

Answers

Activity 1

[1] Adolf Hitler

[2] the Nazi Party, or the Nazis

[3] Mussolini

[4] to make peace with someone by giving that person whatever he wants

[5] blitzkrieg

[6] Winston Churchill

[7] the Soviet Union

[8] Pearl Harbor

[9] Franklin Roosevelt

[10] Possible answers: Britain, France, the Soviet Union, and the United States

[11] Germany, Italy, and Japan

[12] D-Day

[13] the Holocaust

[14] Harry Truman

[15] the atomic bomb

[16] Hiroshima and Nagasaki

Activity 2: Online Interactive Review (Online)

ASSESS

Unit Assessment: World War II (Offline)

Complete an offline Unit Assessment. Your learning coach will score this part of the Assessment.

Name _____ Date _____

World War II

Read each question and its answer choices. Fill in the bubble in front of the word or words that best answer (or complete) the question.

1. Match the name of the person on the left with a description of the country he led during World War II on the right.

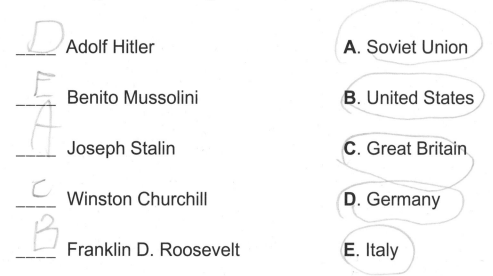

_D_ Adolf Hitler   **A.** Soviet Union

_E_ Benito Mussolini   **B.** United States

_A_ Joseph Stalin   **C.** Great Britain

_C_ Winston Churchill   **D.** Germany

_B_ Franklin D. Roosevelt   **E.** Italy

2. Why did dictators come to power in Europe and Japan in the years following World War I?

  ⓐ People wanted strong leaders to keep complex alliances in place.

  ⓑ People wanted dictators to end the Industrial Revolution for good.

  ⓒ People were looking for strong leaders who promised better times.

  ⓓ People wanted dictators to make sure no single country grew too strong.

3. When Adolf Hitler began taking over territories in Europe, Great Britain and France responded with a policy of appeasement. In other words, they

   (a) tried to keep peace by making Hitler pull his army back.

   (b) began building up their armies and making loud threats.

   (c) began taking over more territories of their own in Europe.

   (d) tried to keep peace by giving Hitler whatever he wanted.

4. What was the name of Adolf Hitler's political party?

   (a) The Red Shirts

   (b) The Nazi Party

   (c) The Communist Party

   (d) The Axis Party

5. What did Great Britain and France do when Adolf Hitler attacked Poland, his neighbor to the east?

   (a) They decided to look the other way again, hoping to avoid a war.

   (b) They finally declared war on Germany, and World War II began.

   (c) They asked the League of Nations to order an end to the attacks.

   (d) They made Germany agree to pay large reparations for the invasion.

6. Hitler used *blitzkrieg* at the outset of World War II. What was *blitzkrieg*?

   (a) False war, using threats and empty promises

   (b) Trench war, using a long series of trenches

   (c) Lightning war, using speed and surprise

   (d) Bombing war, using attacks from the air

7. For Americans, December 7 is known as "Pearl Harbor Day" because of the events of December 7, 1941. How did President Franklin D. Roosevelt describe that day?

   (a) "Our country's darkest hour"

   (b) "The day the whole earth stood still"

   (c) "Our country's finest hour"

   (d) "A date which will live in infamy"

8. Germany, Italy, and Japan were known as the _____ powers during World War II, and Great Britain, France, the United States, and the Soviet Union were known as the _____ powers.

   (a) Axis; Allied

   (b) Allied; Axis

   (c) Central; Allied

   (d) Allied; Central

9. During World War II, many British parents in London and other big cities decided to send their children to the countryside. Why did they do that?

    (a)   Diseases were sweeping the big cities, and there was a shortage of penicillin.

    (b)   German armies had crossed the English Channel and were invading big cities.

    (c)   The Germans were launching air attacks on cities during the Battle of Britain.

    (d)   Children worked in factories in the countryside to help build British airplanes.

10. What was D-Day?

    (a)   The day the Allies launched an invasion of France across the English Channel.

    (b)   The day Germany surrendered, bringing an end to World War II in Europe.

    (c)   The day Japan surrendered, bringing an end to World War II in the Pacific.

    (d)   The day Germany launched an invasion of Europe and triggered World War II.

11. Who was Dwight D. Eisenhower?

   ⓐ   The American president who made the decision to drop the atomic bomb.

   ⓧ ⓑ   The British prime minister who led his country during its darkest hour.

   ⓒ   The British general who insisted that Hitler must be stopped, regardless of the cost.

   ⓓ   The American commander who led the invasion of Europe from Great Britain.

12. As the Allies pushed toward Germany, they saw evidence of one of the greatest horrors of World War II. Today we remember it as the Holocaust. What was the Holocaust?

   ⓐ   The bombing of German cities by British and American war planes

   ⓑ   The mass murder of millions of Jews by the Nazis

   ⓒ   The starvation of millions of Russians on the orders of Joseph Stalin

   ⓓ   The destruction of cities by Adolf Hitler's armies

13. Anne Frank is now one of the most famous names of World War II. This Jewish girl showed courage and hope while doing which of the following?

   (a) Hiding from the Nazis with her family

   (b) Fighting the Germans as a French soldier

   (c) Serving as a spy in the Netherlands

   (d) Escaping from a Nazi concentration camp

14. Who became President after Franklin Roosevelt and made the decision to drop the atomic bomb?

   (a) Dwight D. Eisenhower

   (b) George Marshall

   (c) Harry Truman

   (d) Woodrow Wilson

15. On which two cities did the United States drop atomic bombs during World War II?

   (a) Tokyo and Hiroshima

   (b) Berlin and Tokyo

   (c) Hiroshima and Nagasaki

   (d) Berlin and Moscow

16. What happened after the United States used the atomic bomb in World War II?

   (a)   Germany and Japan formed a new alliance against the United States.

   (b)   Japan surrendered, bringing an end to the war in the Pacific.

   (c)   Japan fought back, causing the war to drag on for months.

   (d)   Germany and the Soviet Union both surrendered to the United States.

17. Essay Question

Write a brief essay about Pearl Harbor. Start with this topic sentence: Americans will long remember the events of December 7, 1941.

Include the following:
* Tell where Pearl Harbor is located.
* Describe what the Japanese did at Pearl Harbor.
* Tell what the United States did after the events at Pearl Harbor.

_____

_____

_____

_____

_____

_____

_____

Student Guide
Lesson 1: Lending a Hand with the Marshall Plan

When World War II ended, people hoped to build a better world. Instead a new kind of war broke out--a Cold War. It was a tense, dangerous time as two world superpowers faced off against each other. But it was also a time of remarkable achievements in science. And, as it turned out, it was a time when freedom gained new life across the globe.

The victors in World War II wanted a lasting peace. They would help rebuild the war-torn nations of Europe as well as Japan. The Marshall Plan helped feed and rebuild Europe.

Lesson Objectives

- Describe some ways nations attempted to rebuild a better world after World War II and identify some of the people who worked for these changes (Marshall Plan, formation of the United Nations, Declaration of Universal Human Rights, Harry Truman, George Marshall, Eleanor Roosevelt).
- Explain that after the second world war many colonial empires collapsed and name Ghandi as the leader of Indian independence.
- Describe the Cold War as a post-war struggle between the United States and the Soviet Union, between democratic and communist nations.
- Identify the build up of nuclear weapons as the greatest fear and threat to peace.
- Identify some of the key figures, symbols, and events of the Cold War (Stalin, Truman, Mao Ze Dong, John F. Kennedy, the Berlin Wall, Ronald Reagan).
- Explain that the post-war period was a time of advance in medicine and technology and name some of these advances (such as polio vaccine, lunar landing and space travel).
- Explain that the Cold War ended and the Soviet Union collapsed in 1989 when the Berlin Wall fell.
- Describe Europe as a continent in ruins at the end of the Second World War.
- Explain that Harry Truman thought the best chance for lasting peace was to help war-torn nations rebuild with sound economies and democratic governments.
- Describe the Marshall Plan as the U.S. plan to help rebuild Europe.
- Recognize that the Marshall Plan was named after Secretary of State George Marshall.

PREPARE

Approximate lesson time is 60 minutes.

LEARN
Activity 1: Rebuilding Europe *(Online)*

Activity 2: Introducing the Marshall Plan *(Offline)*
Write a speech for Secretary of State Marshall, introducing his plan. Print the Student Guide and get started.

Imagine you work for the U.S. State Department in the years immediately following the Second World War. You're the speechwriter for Secretary of State Marshall. He has asked you to write a speech for him. The speech will be about his plan for rebuilding Europe. He will give the speech to the U.S. Congress. Include the following in the speech:

- Describe conditions in Europe right after World War II.
- Explain why it's important to help rebuild Europe.
- Tell how the U.S. proposes to help rebuild war-torn nations.

Have an adult check your speech. If time permits, gather an audience and give your speech.

ASSESS
Lesson Assessment: Lending a Hand with the Marshall Plan *(Online)*
You will complete an online assessment covering the main objectives of this lesson. Your assessment will be scored by the computer.

Student Guide
Lesson 2: Formation of the United Nations

After the Second World War, people everywhere wanted to avoid another great world war. If nations could meet and discuss their problems, maybe they could keep the peace. The United Nations was formed to promote that goal.

Lesson Objectives
- Describe the United Nations as an international organization formed to promote world peace.
- Explain that the UN was founded at the end of World War II to encourage cooperation among nations.
- Explain that the UN's Universal Declaration of Human Rights spelled out rights for people all over the world.
- Name Eleanor Roosevelt as the person who led the effort to write the Universal Declaration of Human Rights.

PREPARE

Approximate lesson time is 60 minutes.

Materials
For the Student
- 🖳 The United Nations

Keywords and Pronunciation
commission : A group of people who are given a duty to perform.

LEARN
Activity 1: Eleanor Roosevelt and Human Rights *(Online)*

Activity 2: History Journal *(Offline)*
It's time to add another chapter to the story of the past. Follow the directions to complete a new entry in your History Journal.

Turn to a new page in your History Journal. On this page, write a short paragraph. Your paragraph must have the answers to the following questions.
1. What is the United Nations and what was it created to do?
2. After what major war was the United Nations founded?
3. What is the United Nations' Universal Declaration of Human Rights?
4. Who led the effort to write the Universal Declaration of Human Rights?

When you have finished, check your work. Date your entry and label it with the lesson title. It will be used to assess how well you understood the lesson.

Activity 3: The United Nations *(Offline)*

Print and complete the United Nations activity sheet.

ASSESS

Lesson Assessment: Formation of the United Nations (*Online*)

Have an adult review your answers to your History Journal entry and input the results online.

Name _____ Date _____

The United Nations

The United Nations, or U.N., is an international organization that was formed at the end of World War II to promote world peace and encourage cooperation among nations. With such an important and complex job to do, the United Nations is, by necessity, a very large organization.

The U.N. is divided into six principal organs as shown below. Think of them as departments within the organization. Select three and use an encyclopedia to help you describe their roles in the United Nations.

The United Nations System

International Court of Justice	Security Council	General Assembly
Economic and Social Council	Trusteeship Council	Secretariat

1. Organ: _____

   Its role in the U.N.:

   _____

   _____

   _____

2. Organ: _____

    Its role in the U.N.:

    _____

    _____

    _____

3. Organ: _____

    Its role in the U.N.:

    _____

    _____

    _____

Lesson Assessment

Formation of the United Nations

Your student was asked the following questions in the Lesson's History Journal entry. Evaluate your student's responses in the activity and input the results online.

1. What is the United Nations and what was it created to do?

2. After what major war was the United Nations founded?

3. What is the United Nations' Universal Declaration of Human Rights?

4. Who led the effort to write the Universal Declaration of Human Rights?

Student Guide
Lesson 3: End of Empires: Gandhi in India

After World War II, many nations that were under colonial rule wanted independence. Mohandas Gandhi helped free India from British rule. He is considered the father of the nation of India.

Lesson Objectives

- Explain that India had been ruled by Great Britain.
- Identify Mohandas Gandhi as the leader of the movement for Indian independence.
- Explain that Gandhi used peaceful resistance to oppose British rule, and give one example of that technique (such as fasting, the Salt March, or wearing Indian cloth instead of British cloth).
- Explain that after World War II, European colonial empires began to disappear.

PREPARE

Approximate lesson time is 60 minutes.

Materials
> For the Student
>> globe

Keywords and Pronunciation
Dandi (dahn-dee)
khadi (kah-dee)
Mohandas Gandhi (MOH-huhn-dahs GAHN-dee)

LEARN
Activity 1: The Nonviolent Fight for Indian Independence *(Online)*
Mohandas Gandhi believed in human dignity and the power of the people. He did not believe in violence. Read about what Gandhi did for India, Britain, and the world.

Activity 2: Gandhi Opposes British Rule *(Offline)*
Gandhi helped India win its independence from Britain without firing a shot. Explain how in a short writing assignment.

After World War II, many nations that had been under colonial rule wanted independence. Mohandas Gandhi helped free India from British rule. He is considered the father of the nation of India.
Write two paragraphs about Gandhi and his efforts to free India from British rule. In the first paragraph, explain how Gandhi used peaceful resistance to gain Indian independence. In the second paragraph, explain why you think peaceful resistance worked.
Have an adult check your work.

ASSESS
Lesson Assessment: End of Empires: Gandhi in India (*Online*)
You will complete an online assessment covering the main objectives of this lesson. Your assessment will be scored by the computer.

LEARN
Activity 3. Optional: End of Empires: Gandhi in India (*Offline*)
From tea party to salt march--what did the American and Indian drives for independence have in common?

In the 1790s, an American poet looked ahead to the days when "the children of India too, will lose the shackles that bind them."

The American and Indian drives for independence were separated by almost 200 years. Yet there are some similarities between the two. Think about what you learned in this lesson and in previous lessons on the American Revolution. You might need to revisit those lessons.

In your History Journal, compare these two independence movements.

Student Guide
Lesson 4: The Cold War and the Berlin Wall

World War II had ended, but now a Cold War began between two new superpowers, the United States and the Soviet Union. Americans worried about the Iron Curtain the Soviets had drawn over Eastern Europe. Within Eastern Europe, people still struggled for freedom and self-rule.

Lesson Objectives

- Describe the Cold War as a dangerous period of rivalry between the United States and the Soviet Union.
- Explain that as chief rivals in the Cold War, the Soviet Union led communist nations and the United States led democratic nations.
- Explain that each side built nuclear weapons, which implied the threat of a third world war.
- Explain that the Berlin Wall was a wall erected by communists to keep people in East Berlin.

PREPARE

Approximate lesson time is 60 minutes.

Materials

For the Student
Optional

- 🖥 Map of Europe
- 🖥 Geography of the Cold War
- 🖥 Map of Cold War Europe, 1962

The Fall of the Berlin Wall: The Cold War Ends by Nigel Kelly

Keywords and Pronunciation

Czechoslovakia (cheh-kuh-sloh-VAH-kee-uh)

LEARN
Activity 1: A War and a Wall (Online)

Activity 2: History Journal (Offline)

It's time to add another chapter to the story of the past. Follow the directions to complete a new entry in your History Journal.

Turn to a new page in your History Journal. On this page, write a paragraph that tells what the lesson was about.

Begin with a topic sentence that introduces the paragraph. Include at least three sentences that give details about the lesson. End with a concluding sentence. You may use the Show You Know questions to help you get started.

When you have finished, check your work. Make sure you have written in complete sentences. Check to make sure you used correct capitalization and punctuation. Date your entry and label it with the lesson title.

Guided Learning: Compare your paragraph with the one in the Teacher Guide.

Activity 3: Geography of the Cold War *(Offline)*

Print and complete the Geography of the Cold War activity sheet. You'll need the map of Cold War Europe, 1962, to complete this activity.

ASSESS

Lesson Assessment: The Cold War and the Berlin Wall (*Online*)

You will complete an online assessment covering the main objectives of this lesson. Your assessment will be scored by the computer.

LEARN

Activity 4. Optional: The Cold War and the Berlin Wall *(Offline)*

For a look ahead, read about the fall of the Berlin Wall and the end of the Cold War in *The Fall of the Berlin Wall: The Cold War Ends,* by Nigel Kelly (Heinemann Library, 2001).

Cold War Europe, 1962

Communist bloc countries

ICELAND

NORWAY
Oslo

SWEDEN
Stockholm

FINLAND
Helsinki
Leningrad

North Sea

DENMARK
Copenhagen

Baltic Sea

SOVIET UNION
Minsk

IRELAND
Dublin

UNITED KINGDOM

London

NETHER-LANDS
Amsterdam

Brussels

BELGIUM

Hamburg
Bremen
Hanover

EAST GERMANY
Berlin

Leipzig

Bonn

POLAND
Warsaw

Kiev

ATLANTIC OCEAN

Paris

LUX.

Frankfurt

Prague

CZECHOSLOVAKIA

WEST GERMANY

Munich

Vienna
Salzburg

Budapest

HUNGARY

FRANCE

SWITZ.

Geneva

AUSTRIA

ROMANIA

Bucharest

YUGOSLAVIA
Sarajevo

SPAIN
Madrid

Rome
ITALY

BULGARIA

Istanbul

ALBANIA

TURKEY

GREECE
Athens

Mediterranean Sea

0   200   400 mi
0   200   400 km

Name _____   Date _____

Geography of the Cold War

After World War II, Americans feared the Soviets would try to take over other countries and make them communist. The United States began to arm itself against the potential threat. In response, the Soviet Union began to build up its own arsenal of weapons.

1. What was this dangerous period of rivalry between the United States and the Soviet Union called?

   _____

One reason this period of time was so dangerous is that the United States and the Soviet Union began developing special kinds of weapons. The weapons implied a threat of a third world war.

2. What kind of weapons did the United States and the Soviet Union develop?

   _____

The rivalry between the United States and the Soviet Union continued to grow. It was a dangerous time of mistrust.

3. During this time, the United States led _____ nations, and the

   Soviet Union led _____ nations.

4. Use the map of Cold War Europe, 1962, to list the nations in Europe that were allied with the United States, and list the communist countries that were under Soviet influence.

American Allies	Under Soviet Influence
_____	_____
_____	_____
_____	_____
_____	_____

Germany was a special case in post-war Europe. All other countries on the continent were either allied with the United States or under Soviet influence. Germany, however, was divided after the war. The eastern half of the country became East Germany and was under Soviet influence. The western half became West Germany, established a democratic government, and became an ally of the United States.

Deep inside Communist East Germany was Berlin, its capital. Like Germany, Berlin was divided—West Berlin and East Berlin. West Berlin was part of West Germany and was protected by Allied troops who had arrived at the end of World War II.

5. What did the communists in East Berlin do to keep people from leaving East Berlin?

_____

Cold War Europe, 1962

Communist bloc countries

ICELAND

ATLANTIC OCEAN

North Sea

Baltic Sea

NORWAY
Oslo

SWEDEN
Stockholm

FINLAND
Helsinki

SOVIET UNION
Leningrad
Minsk
Kiev

IRELAND
Dublin

UNITED KINGDOM
London

DENMARK
Copenhagen

Hamburg
Bremen
Amsterdam
Hanover

NETHERLANDS

Brussels
BELGIUM
Bonn
Frankfurt
LUX.

EAST GERMANY
Berlin
Leipzig

WEST GERMANY

POLAND
Warsaw

Paris

FRANCE

SWITZ.
Geneva

Munich
Salzburg
AUSTRIA
Vienna

CZECHOSLOVAKIA
Prague

HUNGARY
Budapest

ROMANIA
Bucharest

YUGOSLAVIA
Sarajevo

BULGARIA

SPAIN
Madrid

Rome
ITALY

ALBANIA

Istanbul

TURKEY

GREECE
Athens

Mediterranean Sea

0   200   400 mi
0   200   400 km

Student Guide
Lesson 5: Mao Zedong in China

Soon after World War II ended, China also turned to communism. China's leader, Mao Zedong (or Mao), kept a tight control over the Chinese people. He even tried to control what they thought. With his Great Cultural Revolution, Mao silenced all who did not agree with his ideas.

Lesson Objectives

- Describe Mao Zedong as the leader who made China a Communist nation.
- Describe Mao's tight control over China.
- Explain that the Cultural Revolution was an attempt to silence those who did not agree with Mao's ideas.

PREPARE

Approximate lesson time is 60 minutes.

Materials

For the Student

globe

🖳 Mao's Ever Present Face

Keywords and Pronunciation

Hu Meiping (hoo may-ping)

Mao Zedong (maou dzuh-doung)

Zhang Sing-Nan (jahng shing-ahn)

LEARN

Activity 1: Chairman Mao (Online)

Mao pushed China hard to become a modern industrialized nation. For better or for worse, he made his mark on China.

Activity 2: History Journal (Offline)

It's time to add another chapter to the story of the past. Follow the directions to complete a new entry in your History Journal.

Turn to a new page in your History Journal. On this page, write a paragraph that tells what the lesson was about.

Begin with a topic sentence that introduces the paragraph. Include at least three sentences that give details about the lesson. End with a concluding sentence. You may use the Show You Know questions to help you get started.

When you have finished, check your work. Make sure you have written in complete sentences. Check to make sure you used correct capitalization and punctuation. Date your entry and label it with the lesson title.

Guided Learning: Compare your paragraph with the one in the Teacher Guide.

Activity 3: Mao's Ever Present Face (*Offline*)

Print and complete the Mao's Ever Present Face activity sheet. Have an adult check your work.

ASSESS

Lesson Assessment: Mao Zedong in China (*Online*)

You will complete an online assessment covering the main objectives of this lesson. Your assessment will be scored by the computer.

Name _____ Date _____

Mao's Ever Present Face

Now, many years after Mao Zedong's death, his face still appears all over China. He is a symbol of modern China and its Communist revolution.

Read each statement that follows. If the statement is true, paste a picture of Mao's face in the space provided. Note: If any part of the statement is not true, do not paste the picture in the space.

1. Mao Zedong was born into a wealthy, prosperous family and grew up to be a revolutionary.

2. Mao believed that communism was the answer to the world's problems.

3. Mao was the leader who made China a Democratic nation.

4. Mao fought against the Soviet army's Red Guard.

5. The Cultural Revolution was an attempt to silence those who did not agree with Mao's ideas.

6. One way in which Mao kept tight control over China was to arrest scientists, doctors, and teachers, and to send them to prison.

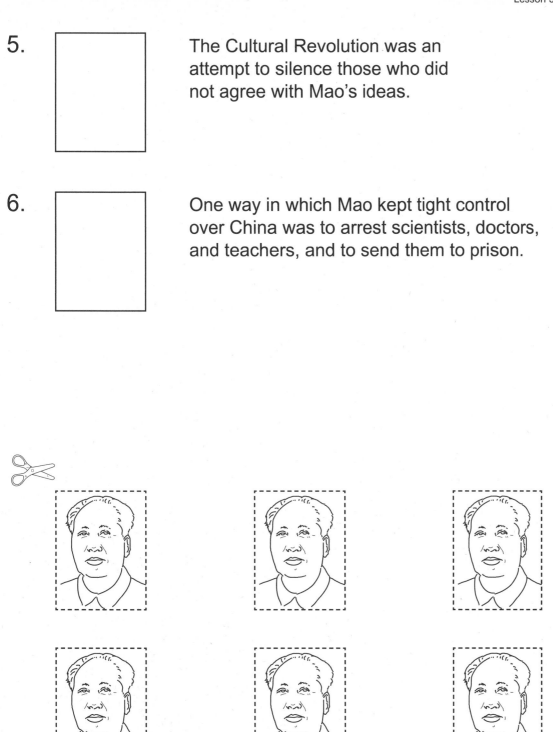

Student Guide
Lesson 6: Defeating Polio

Polio was a disease that struck thousands every year. Many victims were left crippled. Many of those victims were children. In the 1950s, the American scientist Jonas Salk devoted himself to finding a polio vaccine. His work helped rid the world of this terrible disease.

Lesson Objectives

- Describe polio as a disease that struck thousands of people every year.
- Describe polio as a disease that paralyzed or crippled many of its victims.
- Identify Jonas Salk as the creator of a vaccine to prevent polio.
- Explain that polio ceased to be a threat when the vaccine was given in childhood.

PREPARE

Approximate lesson time is 60 minutes.

Materials

> For the Student
>
>> Jonas Salk and the Polio Vaccine by John Bankston

Keywords and Pronunciation

epidemic : An outbreak of disease among many people.

virus : Microscopic organisms that cause diseases.

LEARN
Activity 1: The Cure for Polio (Online)

Activity 2: Polio Vaccine Invented! (Offline)
Write a newspaper article reporting the invention of the polio vaccine. Your article will be used as today's lesson assessment.

Polio. Great epidemics of the disease that crippled Franklin Delano Roosevelt spread all over the world. It was feared everywhere. But polio was finally defeated when a vaccine was invented. That was BIG news at the time.

Write a newspaper article about polio and the invention of the vaccine. The article should:
- Describe polio--what it is and what it does.
- Explain what a terrible problem polio used to be.
- Identify the inventor of the polio vaccine.
- Tell whether the vaccine is effective in stopping polio.

You can include more information from the lesson in the article, but the article must address those points. The information you provide about them will be assessed.

ASSESS
Lesson Assessment: Defeating Polio (*Online*)

Have an adult review your History Journal essay and input the results in the assessment at the end of the lesson.

LEARN
Activity 3. Optional: Defeating Polio (*Offline*)

Learn more about the inventor of the polio vaccine by reading *Jonas Salk and the Polio Vaccine*, by John Bankston (Mitchell Lane Publishers, 2001).

Name _____   Date _____

Lesson Assessment

Defeating Polio

Polio. Great epidemics of the disease that crippled Franklin Delano Roosevelt spread all over the world. It was feared everywhere. But polio was finally defeated when a vaccine was invented. That was BIG news at the time.

Write a newspaper article about polio and the invention of the vaccine. The article should:

- Describe polio--what it is and what it does.
- Explain what a terrible problem polio used to be.
- Identify the inventor of the polio vaccine.
- Tell whether the vaccine is effective in stopping polio.

You can include more information from the lesson in the article, but the article must address those points.

Student Guide
Lesson 7. Optional: A Computer Revolution

Computers are an important part of modern life. Without computers, for example, you wouldn't be doing this History lesson! Computers are very modern machines, but they didn't simply appear overnight. In fact, their history stretches all the way back to the beginnings of the Scientific Revolution.

Lesson Objectives
- Recognize that scientists and mathematicians have been building machines to help them calculate and solve problems for hundreds of years.
- Explain that in the twentieth century powerful computers that can store large amounts of information and do complex calculations quickly were developed.
- Give an example of how computers help people solve problems or communicate faster than ever before.

PREPARE

Approximate lesson time is 60 minutes.

Keywords and Pronunciation
Blaise Pascal (blez pahs-KAHL)
census : A count of the population.
Colossus (kuh-LAH-suhs)
compute : To make calculations
Joseph-Marie Jacquard (zhoh-zef ma-REE zhah-kahr)
Pascaline (PA-skuh-liyn)
UNIVAC (YOO-nih-vac)

LEARN
Activity 1. Optional: Optional Lesson Instructions *(Online)*
This lesson is OPTIONAL. It is provided for students who seek enrichment or extra practice. You may skip this lesson.

If you choose to skip this lesson, then go to the Plan or Lesson Lists page and mark this lesson "Skipped" in order to proceed to the next lesson in the course.

Activity 2. Optional: A Computer Family Album *(Online)*

Activity 3. Optional: History Journal *(Offline)*

It's time to add another chapter to the story of the past. Follow the directions to complete a new entry in your History Journal.

Turn to a new page in your History Journal. On this page, write a paragraph that tells what the lesson was about.

Begin with a topic sentence that introduces the paragraph. Include at least three sentences that give details about the lesson. End with a concluding sentence. You may use the Show You Know questions to help you get started.

When you have finished, check your work. Make sure you have written in complete sentences. Check to make sure you used correct capitalization and punctuation. Date your entry and label it with the lesson title.

Guided Learning: Compare your paragraph with the one in the Teacher Guide.

Activity 4. Optional: The World of Computers *(Online)*

Activity 5. Optional: A Computer Revolution *(Online)*

Student Guide
Lesson 8: We Will Go to the Moon

President John F. Kennedy wanted Americans to go to the moon. He said the United States would land a man there, "not because it is easy, but because it is hard." In 1969 Neil Armstrong stood on the surface of the moon, and the world was suddenly a lot smaller.

Lesson Objectives

- Explain that the space age began when the Soviet Union launched *Sputnik*, the first man-made satellite to orbit Earth.
- Identify John F. Kennedy as the president who committed the United States to landing a man on the moon.
- Identify the Apollo program as the U.S. space program that put a man on the moon, and recognize the Apollo 11 mission as the first to reach the moon.
- Name Neil Armstrong as the first person to walk on the moon.

PREPARE

Approximate lesson time is 60 minutes.

Keywords and Pronunciation
satellite : An object that orbits a planet.
Sputnik (SPUT-nik)

LEARN
Activity 1: A Man on the Moon *(Online)*

Activity 2: History Journal *(Offline)*
It's time to add another chapter to the story of the past. Follow the directions to complete a new entry in your History Journal.

Turn to a new page in your History Journal. On this page, write a paragraph that tells what the lesson was about.

Begin with a topic sentence that introduces the paragraph. Include at least three sentences that give details about the lesson. End with a concluding sentence. You may use the Show You Know questions to help you get started.

When you have finished, check your work. Make sure you have written in complete sentences. Check to make sure you used correct capitalization and punctuation. Date your entry and label it with the lesson title.

Guided Learning: Compare your paragraph with the one in the Teacher Guide.

Activity 3: To the Moon and Back *(Online)*

ASSESS

Lesson Assessment: We Will Go to the Moon (*Online*)

You will complete an online assessment covering the main objectives of this lesson. Your assessment will be scored by the computer.

LEARN
Activity 4. Optional: We Will Go to the Moon *(Online)*

Student Guide
Lesson 9. Optional: A Polish Pope and Eastern Europe

Poland was one of the nations behind the Iron Curtain during the Cold War. Communists robbed the Polish people of many freedoms, including the freedom to worship God. In 1979 a Polish pope named John Paul II visited his homeland. It was a visit that challenged communist rule and helped change the world.

Lesson Objectives
- Locate Poland on a map.
- Describe John Paul II as a Polish pope.
- Explain that the pope's trip to Poland encouraged the Polish people to resist communist rule.

PREPARE

Approximate lesson time is 60 minutes.

Materials
For the Student
- Cold War Europe, 1962

Keywords and Pronunciation
Karol Wojtyla (KAH-ruhl voy-TIL-ah)

Pole : Someone who lives in Poland.

pope : The leader of the Catholic Church.

strike : Stopping work as a way of protesting against something you think is wrong.

union : A group that protects the rights of workers.

LEARN
Activity 1. Optional: Optional Lesson Instructions *(Online)*

This lesson is OPTIONAL. It is provided for students who seek enrichment or extra practice. You may skip this lesson.

If you choose to skip this lesson, then go to the Plan or Lesson Lists page and mark this lesson "Skipped" in order to proceed to the next lesson in the course.

Activity 2. Optional: Poland Under Soviet Rule *(Online)*

Read how Pope John Paul II inspired the people of Poland to believe in themselves and their faith and resist communist rule.

Activity 3. Optional: A Letter *(Offline)*

Write a letter to a friend about Pope John Paul's visit to Poland.

Imagine it's 1979 and you are Polish: write a letter to a friend telling about Pope John Paul's visit to Poland. Include the following in your letter:

- Explain why everyone was so excited about the pope's visit.
- Tell what you hope will result from the pope's visit.

Cold War Europe, 1962

Communist bloc countries

N

ICELAND

NORWAY
Oslo

SWEDEN
Stockholm

FINLAND
Helsinki
Leningrad

SOVIET UNION

North Sea

DENMARK
Copenhagen

Baltic Sea

IRELAND
Dublin

UNITED KINGDOM

London

NETHER-LANDS
Amsterdam

Brussels
BELGIUM

Hamburg
Bremen
Hanover

EAST GERMANY
Berlin
Leipzig

Minsk

Warsaw

POLAND

Kiev

Bonn

Frankfurt

Prague
CZECHOSLOVAKIA

ATLANTIC OCEAN

Paris

LUX.

WEST GERMANY

Munich

Vienna
Salzburg
AUSTRIA

Budapest

HUNGARY

ROMANIA

FRANCE

SWITZ.

Geneva

Bucharest

YUGOSLAVIA
Sarajevo

BULGARIA

SPAIN

Madrid

Rome
ITALY

ALBANIA

Istanbul

TURKEY

GREECE

Athens

Mediterranean Sea

0   200   400 mi
0   200   400 km

Student Guide
Lesson 10: The End of the Cold War

The Berlin Wall stood for decades as the most famous symbol of communist rule. In a speech in West Berlin, U.S. President Ronald Reagan challenged the Soviets to tear it down. The Wall was finally knocked down in 1989, bringing an end to the long Cold War.

Lesson Objectives

- Identify Ronald Reagan as the U.S. president who challenged the communists to tear down the Berlin Wall.
- State that the Cold War ended in 1989 when the Berlin Wall fell.
- Explain that the Soviet Union's communist empire collapsed and democracy came to Eastern Europe.

PREPARE

Approximate lesson time is 60 minutes.

Materials

For the Student

    History Journal

    💻 After the Cold War

    map, world

Keywords and Pronunciation

Mikhail Gorbachev (mih-kah-EEL gawr-buh-CHAWF)

LEARN
Activity 1: The Cold War Begins to Thaw *(Online)*

Activity 2: History Journal *(Offline)*

It's time to add another chapter to the story of the past. Follow the directions to complete a new entry in your History Journal.

Turn to a new page in your History Journal. On this page, write a paragraph that tells what the lesson was about.

Begin with a topic sentence that introduces the paragraph. Include at least three sentences that give details about the lesson. End with a concluding sentence. You may use the Show You Know questions to help you get started.

When you have finished, check your work. Make sure you have written in complete sentences. Check to make sure you used correct capitalization and punctuation. Date your entry and label it with the lesson title.

Guided Learning: Compare your paragraph with the one in the Teacher Guide.

Activity 3: After the Cold War *(Online)*

Print and complete the After the Cold War activity sheet. You'll need your place mat map of the World to complete the activity. You'll also need to view this online map.

ASSESS

Lesson Assessment: The End of the Cold War (*Online*)

You will complete an online assessment covering the main objectives of this lesson. Your assessment will be scored by the computer.

Name _____   Date _____

After the Cold War

The fall of the Berlin Wall was just the beginning of the end of communism in Eastern Europe. Like the Berlin Wall, communism itself started to collapse. The Soviet Union's empire fell apart. Even the Soviet Union ceased to exist. The largest republic in the empire went back to being called "Russia." The other republics in the old Soviet Union established their own governments and became new nations.

Use your place mat map of the world and the online map of Comparative Soviet Nationalities by Republic to answer questions 4 - 6. Note: The letters "S.S.R." used on the online map stand for "Soviet Socialist Republic."

1. Who challenged the communists in East Germany to tear down the Berlin

   Wall? _____

2. What Eastern European nation first challenged the Soviets, pushing for free elections and democracy? _____

3. In what year did the Cold War end? _____

4.   After the collapse of the Soviet Union, the Russian Soviet Federative

   Socialist Republic became the country of _____.

5. How many republics became independent nations after the collapse of the

   Soviet Union? _____

6. Name the new nations: _____

_____

_____

_____

_____

Student Guide
Lesson 11: Unit Review and Assessment

You've completed this unit, and now it's time to review what you've learned and take the unit assessment.

Lesson Objectives

- Demonstrate mastery of important knowledge and skills in this unit.
- Explain that Harry Truman thought the best chance for lasting peace was to help war-torn nations rebuild with sound economies and democratic governments.
- Describe the Marshall Plan as the U.S. plan to help rebuild Europe.
- Describe the United Nations as an international organization formed to promote world peace.
- Explain that the UN was founded at the end of World War II to encourage cooperation among nations.
- Name Eleanor Roosevelt as the person who led the effort to write the Universal Declaration of Human Rights.
- Identify Mohandas Gandhi as the leader of the movement for Indian independence.
- Explain that Gandhi used peaceful resistance to oppose British rule, and give one example of that technique (such as fasting, the Salt March, or wearing Indian cloth instead of British cloth).
- Explain that after World War II, European colonial empires began to disappear.
- Describe the Cold War as a dangerous period of rivalry between the United States and the Soviet Union.
- Explain that as chief rivals in the Cold War, the Soviet Union led communist nations and the United States led democratic nations.
- Explain that each side built nuclear weapons, which implied the threat of a third world war.
- Explain that the Berlin Wall was a wall erected by communists to keep people in East Berlin.
- Describe Mao Zedong as the leader who made China a Communist nation.
- Identify Jonas Salk as the creator of a vaccine to prevent polio.
- Identify John F. Kennedy as the president who committed the United States to landing a man on the moon.
- Name Neil Armstrong as the first person to walk on the moon.
- Identify Ronald Reagan as the U.S. president who challenged the communists to tear down the Berlin Wall.
- State that the Cold War ended in 1989 when the Berlin Wall fell.
- Explain that the Soviet Union's communist empire collapsed and democracy came to Eastern Europe.
- Explain that the post-war period was a time of advance in medicine and technology and name some of these advances (such as polio vaccine, lunar landing and space travel).

PREPARE

Approximate lesson time is 60 minutes.

LEARN
Activity 1: Rebuilding a Better World (Offline)

We've covered a lot, and now it's time to take a look back. Here's what you should remember about Rebuilding a Better World.

After World War II leaders of the world's democracies faced tough questions. How could they create a more peaceful world? How could they make sure atomic weapons would not be used? How could they make the world a healthier place? How could they spread freedom? They didn't solve every problem, but the world they shaped was a lot better than the world they were born into.

How could people stop a war like World War II from ever happening again? Harry Truman, President of the United States, had a good idea. He said the United States should lend a hand to those in need.

By 1945 many nations lay in ruins. Homes, shops, factories, schools, and roads were destroyed in Europe and Asia. The Germans and the Japanese were among the hardest hit. President Truman and Secretary of State George Marshall said that to create a more peaceful world, the U.S. should help its friends and former enemies recover. Those nations had to rebuild and create new democracies of their own. They needed help. What was the name of the plan Harry Truman suggested to help nations rebuild? [1]

Leaders of the world also decided that nations needed a place to come together and talk about their problems. They needed an international organization to encourage peace. What is the name of the organization they started after World War II to help promote peace? [2]

Who was one of America's first representatives to the United Nations? [3]

Eleanor Roosevelt thought people shouldn't talk just about their differences. They should also talk about their common hopes and ideals, about the rights every human being deserved. What Declaration did Eleanor Roosevelt help the U.N. write? [4]

The Universal Declaration of Human Rights said flat-out that all people had the right to be free and to choose their own leaders. It gave democracy a leg-up in the world.

Soon the great colonial empires realized their days were numbered. Once people had said that "the sun never sets on the British empire." Now the British began to free the colonies in that empire. What former British colony in Asia became independent after World War II? [5]

What famous lawyer led the non-violent movement for independence there? [6]

Other colonies under other nations gained their freedom, too. Africa went from being a colonized continent to the home of more than 40 independent nations.

Freedom wasn't gaining everywhere, though. The Soviet Union, a great communist power, controlled much of Eastern Europe. What was the name of the dictator who led the Soviet Union at this time? [7]

Stalin made sure there were no free elections behind the Iron Curtain. There was no free press. There was no freedom of religion. Those lands suffered under communist rule.

The United States and Soviet Union did not go to war against each other and they did not use their atomic weapons, but it was a time of great tension. What was the name of this "non-shooting war" between the United States and the Soviet Union? [8]

What were people most afraid of during the Cold War? [9]

During the Cold War, one huge Asian country became communist. Which nation was that? [10]

What is the name of the leader who ruled China during this time? [11]

The communists made sure that they alone ruled. In China, Mao began a great "Cultural Revolution." He arrested any who disagreed with him or what he had done. In East Germany the communists couldn't arrest everyone. Instead they built a wall to keep their citizens inside. Guards and barbed wire ensured that no one crossed into the west. This wall, which divided one of Germany's great cities, became a symbol of the Cold War. What was that wall's name? [12]

There were other symbols of the Cold War, and not all of them were bad. The Soviet Union and the United States entered the space age. Each country wanted to understand more about the heavens and they raced to do it. The Soviets put Sputnik, the first man-made satellite into space. Then they launched the first human being into space.

An American president was worried. He thought the space race was one race the United States better not lose. What was the name of the president who promised the United States would land a man on the moon by the end of the 60s? [13]

John F. Kennedy launched the Apollo space program, dedicated to putting a man on the moon. In 1969, human beings around the world watched the first person set foot on the moon. Who was that person? [14]

As you can see, science and technology had taken big leaps forward in this period. Doctors were learning more and more about disease and how to control it. Jonas Salk invented a vaccine to stop a deadly disease that had crippled Franklin D. Roosevelt and many other people. What was that vaccine? [15]

Meanwhile, engineers were figuring out ways to communicate faster and better. What big invention made it possible for people all over the world to watch the lunar landing? [16]

What invention helped make the lunar landing possible and now keeps the whole world inter-connected? [17]

This story of the years after World War II, the Cold War, and the struggle to rebuild a better world had an amazing ending. People love freedom. And they seek it when they don't have it. Sometimes people just need brave leaders to say, "Keep looking! Push harder! You are right to seek freedom." Then they accomplish astonishing things. What brave Polish pope encouraged people behind the Iron Curtain to do that? [18]

What American President encouraged East Berliners to stand up for freedom and urged Soviet leaders to "tear down this wall"? [19]

When the Berlin Wall fell in 1989, the world watched in awe. The Cold War was over. It had been two hundred years since the American Constitution and the French Revolution. Now two centuries later, freedom had new life. Some years after World War II Harry Truman said: "The whole object was to make the world a fairer and better place." In 1989, in one shining moment, his wish and the wishes of all who cherish freedom came true.

Answers

Activity 1

[1] the Marshall Plan

[2] the United Nations

[3] Eleanor Roosevelt

[4] the Universal Declaration of Human Rights

[5] India

[6] Gandhi

[7] Joseph Stalin

[8] the Cold War

[9] a nuclear war

[10] China

[11] Mao or Mao Zedong

[12] the Berlin Wall

[13] John F. Kennedy

[14] Neil Armstrong

[15] the polio vaccine

[16] television

[17] computers

[18] Pope John Paul II

[19] Ronald Reagan

Activity 2: Online Interactive Review (Online)

ASSESS

Unit Assessment: Rebuilding a Better World (Offline)

Complete an offline Unit Assessment. Your learning coach will score this part of the Assessment.

☼ **Assessment**

Name _____ Date _____

Rebuilding a Better World

Match the name of each person on the left with the correct description on the right. Write the correct letter on the blank line.

1. ___ Eleanor Roosevelt   A. led the Soviet Union during much of the
Cold War

  ___ Mohandas Gandhi   B. committed the United States to landing
a man on the moon

  ___ Joseph Stalin   C. led the effort to write the U.N.
Declaration of Human Rights

  ___ Mao Zedong   D. led the movement for Indian
independence

  ___ John F. Kennedy   E. made China a communist nation

2. How did the Marshall Plan help war-torn nations?

  ⓐ   It built up their armies and fought the Soviet Union.

  ⓑ   It rebuilt their economies and strengthened democracy.

  ⓒ   It brought new dictators to power and spread communism.

  ⓓ   It allowed new colonies in Asia, Africa, and South America.

3. What did the United Nations Declaration of Human Rights do?

    ⓐ   It spelled out the rights that people all over the world
         should have.

    ⓑ   It spelled out terms for peace for all nations after World
         War II.

    ⓒ   It spelled out human rights for people in the Industrial
         Revolution.

    ⓓ   It spelled out human rights for all nations after World War I.

4. How did Mohandas Gandhi lead India to independence from
    Great Britain?

    ⓐ   By using "blood and iron" against the British

    ⓑ   By keeping British ships out of India's ports

    ⓒ   By wearing British clothes to show friendship

    ⓓ   By resisting British rule without violence

5. Which of the following statements is true?

    ⓐ   After World War II, Europeans founded more colonies in
         Africa.

    ⓑ   After World War II, European colonial empires began to
         grow.

    ⓒ   After World War II, European colonial empires began to
         break up.

    ⓓ   After World War II, Europe's colonies started the United
         Nations.

6. Which of the following best describes the Cold War?

   ⓐ A dangerous time of rivalry between the United States and the Soviet Union

   ⓑ A time when the United States and the Soviet Union fought with computers

   ⓒ A period when the rivalry between the United States and the Soviet Union ended

   ⓓ A dangerous time of nuclear war between the United States and the Soviet Union

7. Which of the following caused the greatest fear and was a threat to peace during the Cold War?

   ⓐ Large outbreaks of polio

   ⓑ The race to put men into space

   ⓒ The invention of new computers

   ⓓ The build-up of nuclear weapons

8. During the Cold War, the Soviet Union led _____ nations, while the United States led _____ nations.

   ⓐ democratic; communist

   ⓑ communist; democratic

   ⓒ colonial; communist

   ⓓ democratic; colonial

9. During the Cold War, China became a _____ country.

(a) democratic

(b) communist

(c) colonial

(d) Catholic

10. Why did the communists build the Berlin Wall?

(a) To keep the Soviet Union from sending more troops into East Berlin

(b) To keep people in democratic West Berlin from escaping to East Berlin

(c) To keep people in communist East Berlin from escaping to West Berlin

(d) To keep the United States from taking territory inside East Berlin

11. Which astronaut became the f rst person to set foot on the moon?

(a) Edwin "Buzz" Aldrin

(b) Neil Armstrong

(c) Jonas Salk

(d) George Marshall

12. What is Jonas Salk famous for?

    ⓐ   Coining the phrase "Iron Curtain"

    ⓑ   Developing an early computer

    ⓒ   Walking on the moon

    ⓓ   Creating a polio vaccine

13. What was the name of the president who promised the United States would land an astronaut on the moon by the end of 1960s?

    ⓐ   Franklin Roosevelt

    ⓑ   Harry Truman

    ⓒ   John F. Kennedy

    ⓓ   Ronald Reagan

14. Which famous words did President Ronald Reagan say?

    ⓐ   "The buck stops here!"

    ⓑ   "That's one giant leap for mankind!"

    ⓒ   "An Iron Curtain has descended across Europe!"

    ⓓ   "Mr. Gorbachev, tear down this wall!"

15. When the Cold War ended in 1989, which of the following happened?

    ⓐ   The Berlin Wall fell and the Soviet Union soon collapsed.

    ⓑ   The Berlin Wall fell and communism spread across Europe.

    ⓒ   The communists triumphed and built a new Berlin Wall.

    ⓓ   The United States and Soviet Union repaired the Berlin Wall.

16. Which is the correct chronological order for the three events below?

    ⓐ   Fall of Berlin Wall, Marshall Plan, moon landing

    ⓑ   Marshall Plan, fall of Berlin Wall, moon landing

    ⓒ   Moon landing, fall of Berlin Wall, Marshall Plan

    ⓓ   Marshall Plan, moon landing, fall of Berlin Wall

17. Essay Question

Write a paragraph telling how people tried to rebuild a better world after World War II. Begin with the sentence: "After World War II many people worked hard to make the world a better place."

Include the following:
- Tell why the United Nations was founded.
- Give one example of an advance in science or technology and explain why it was important.
- Give an example that shows that many people gained more freedom during these years.

_____

_____

_____

_____

_____

_____

_____

_____

_____

_____

_____

_____

Student Guide
Lesson 12: Final Review and Assessment

You've completed the second semester, so now it's time to take the semester assessment.

Lesson Objectives

- Demonstrate mastery of important knowledge and skills learned this semester.
- Demonstrate mastery of important knowledge and skills in this unit.
- Define *imperialism* as the drive to create empires overseas.
- Recognize Rudyard Kipling as a great British writer who wrote about India.
- Explain that Kipling wrote children's stories.
- Explain that Kipling celebrated the British Empire in his writings.
- Describe Edison as one of the greatest inventors of all time.
- Explain that Ford's assembly line factory made production faster and cheaper.
- State that the first successful flight occurred at Kitty Hawk, North Carolina.
- Describe the Panama Canal as a waterway connecting the Atlantic and Pacific Oceans.
- State that the "the Great War" was the term used to describe World War I.
- Recognize that "make the world safe for democracy" was a United States slogan in World War I and a reason for entering the war.
- Explain that Woodrow Wilson proposed the League of Nations to stop future wars, and that the United States did not join the League.
- Describe the woman's suffrage movement as the movement for the right of women to vote.
- Describe Charles Lindbergh as the first man to fly solo across the Atlantic Ocean.
- Identify Alexander Fleming as the British scientist who discovered penicillin.
- Identify Franklin Delano Roosevelt as president of the United States during the Great Depression.
- Explain that World War I left many problems unsolved and the Great Depression affected the whole world.
- Identify Stalin, Hitler, and Mussolini as dictators who led the Soviet Union, Germany, and Italy.
- Explain that Churchill led Great Britain through the Battle of Britain.
- Describe the Holocaust as the mass murder of millions of Jews by the Nazis.
- Explain that the Japanese launched a surprise attack on the U.S. Naval Base at Pearl Harbor in Hawaii on December 7, 1941.
- Explain that the United States used the atomic bomb on Hiroshima and Nagasaki to end the war.
- Explain that Harry Truman thought the best chance for lasting peace was to help war-torn nations rebuild with sound economies and democratic governments.
- Describe the United Nations as an international organization formed to promote world peace.
- Name Eleanor Roosevelt as the person who led the effort to write the Universal Declaration of Human Rights.
- Explain that Gandhi used peaceful resistance to oppose British rule, and give one example of that technique (such as fasting, the Salt March, or wearing Indian cloth instead of British cloth).
- Identify Jonas Salk as the creator of a vaccine to prevent polio.

- Identify John F. Kennedy as the president who committed the United States to landing a man on the moon.
- Identify Ronald Reagan as the U.S. president who challenged the communists to tear down the Berlin Wall.
- Describe the late nineteenth and early twentieth centuries as an age of invention and enterprise.
- Describe the Russian Revolution as one that involved the overthrow of the czar and the triumph of Communism.

PREPARE

Approximate lesson time is 60 minutes.

LEARN

Activity 1: Rebuilding a Better World (Offline)

We've covered a lot, and now it's time to take a look back. Here's what you should remember from the second semester.

The 20th century began and ended with hope. But in between was the bloodiest century known to humankind. Nations flexed their muscles and snatched at colonies overseas. Then came two horrible world wars and atomic weapons so powerful they could end life on earth.

Still, scientists and engineers improved medicine, technology, and communication. And throughout the 20th century, people fought for freedom in their lands. By the century's end, communism had gone head-to-head with democracy, and democracy had won. Let's take a look back at some of the big ideas and events.

We learned about a time when people felt so proud of their countries, they decided it wasn't enough for them to be ordinary nations. They wanted empires - colonies overseas! What is the drive to build empires called? [1]

Which European nation built the largest empire at this time? [2]

The British weren't alone in their efforts to get colonies. The French and Germans leapt at the chance. Which continent was almost entirely colonized by European nations in 1900? [3]

The French worked with the Egyptians to leave something lasting in Africa. What did they build that connected the Mediterranean and the Red Seas? [4]

Americans didn't want to be left behind in this drive for empire. Which war did they fight to free Cuba and gain colonies overseas? [5]

If Europeans and Americans were scrambling for territory, they were scrambling for ideas and inventions, too. See if you remember some of the new inventions in this "Can-do!" age.

What device used clicks and pauses to transmit messages over wires? [6]

What invention did Alexander Graham Bell give us to transmit the human voice? [7]

What did Thomas Edison invent? [8]

Henry Ford was inspired by Thomas Edison's research laboratory. What did Ford do? [9]

Americans didn't completely steal the show. Which Italian inventor made the radio part of our lives? [10]

Which Frenchman built a huge tower in Paris to commemorate the French Revolution? [11]

Meanwhile, back in the U.S.A., human beings first soared into the air at Kitty Hawk, North Carolina. Who invented that first successful airplane? [12]

If they had been flying over Panama, they might have seen the brand new Panama Canal. What two bodies of water did that canal connect? [13]

With all this success - new inventions, new buildings, new means of transportation - people began to wonder if they could have "successful" wars too. Sound silly? It was. But they wondered, "Can nations have quick conflicts that lead to big gains for the winner?" That overconfidence led to World War I. What was another name for World War I? [14]

A series of alliances triggered this disastrous war. The war lasted four dreadful years and left millions dead. Soldiers fought from trenches. They used new types of weapons such as planes, tanks, and poison gas. People said that World War I would be "the war to end to end all wars" and "the war to make the world safe for democracy." But it wasn't.

For starters, Russia pulled out of the war and set up a new government. Russian revolutionaries overthrew the czar. What kind of government did they establish in his place? [15]

The new communist government was led by Vladmir Lenin. Lenin was followed by another communist dictator who renamed Russia and ruled with an iron hand. Who was that man? [16]

What was Russia now called? [17]

Then along came Germany's Adolph Hitler. Hitler wasn't the only evil genius in the 1930s, but he was the most dangerous. He took advantage of German anger and European weariness of war. He built up a nationalist party determined to make Germany a giant. What was his party called? [18]

Hitler marched his troops into countries that weren't his. He expected the French and British to stand aside and let him. They did. What was that idea of keeping peace with Hitler called? [19]

Pretty soon the Allies discovered appeasement wouldn't work. When Hitler marched into Poland, they declared war to stop him. The world entered an even worse conflict than World War I. What do we call this terrible war Hitler started? [20]

Hitler teamed up with two other nations to form the Axis. Which two nations were they? [21]

Hitler blamed everyone else for Germany's problems. Which group did he blame the most? [22]

Hitler sent millions of Jews to concentration camps to work and to die. What is that mass murder called? [23]

The allies heard rumors of this horror and fought on. Who led Britain through this terrible time? [24]

What event brought the United States into World War II? [25]

What is the name of the U.S. president who led the United States through most of the war? [26]

Which side was Stalin's Soviet Union on during World War II? [27]

Through most of the war, the British and American alliance with Russia was a tough one. At war's end, it got tougher.

D-Day brought victory in Europe, and the atomic bomb brought victory in the Pacific. But then the victors had to figure out how to remake the world. Some huge improvements were made with the Marshall Plan, the United Nations, and independence for former colonies.

Freedom and self-government was an idea that kept spreading. Even before the war, women had won the right to vote in most of the west. Now after the war, India was one of many nations that gained its independence from former European empires. Who led the Indian drive for independence? [28]

But freedom and self-government weren't gaining everywhere. In China, Mao led a revolution, too. He set up a communist dictatorship there. And in Eastern Europe, Joseph Stalin tightened his grip. He made sure that an "Iron Curtain" was drawn around nations under his influence. No free elections for Poland, Czechoslovakia, Romania, Bulgaria or many other eastern European nations.

Which two nations were the leading powers after World War II? [29]

The United States led democratic nations; the Soviet Union led the communist world. They often opposed each other. Both sides built many nuclear weapons. It was a dangerous time. The U.S. and U.S.S.R. never actually fired weapons at each other, but often they seemed on the brink of it. What was this non-shooting standoff between the United States and the Soviet Union called? [30]

What was the name of the wall that became a visible symbol of the Cold War struggle? [31]

We've learned that communism didn't last forever in eastern Europe. A pope from Poland inspired resistance to communist rule. What was his name? [32]

Which American President went to Berlin and called for the Soviets to "tear down this wall?" [33]

By 1989 the Berlin Wall came tumbling down. The Cold War thawed, and democracy began to flower in the soil of eastern Europe. In the Cold War, freedom and democracy triumphed.

But you'll find out that democracy is never an end. It's just a beginning. When people have freedom, they can use it for good or evil. What will come next in this big book of the human story? That chapter is up to you!

Answers

Activity 1

[1] imperialism

[2] Great Britain

[3] Africa

[4] the Suez Canal

[5] the Spanish American War

[6] the telegraph

[7] the telephone

[8] Possible answer: the electric light bulb

[9] He made the Model T. He used the assembly line to make cars quickly and cheaply.

[10] Marconi

[11] Eiffel

[12] the Wright brothers

[13] the Atlantic and the Pacific Oceans

[14] the Great War

[15] a communist government

[16] Josef Stalin

[17] the Soviet Union, or the U.S.S.R.

[18] the Nazi Party

[19] appeasement

[20] World War II

[21] Italy and Japan

[22] the Jews

[23] the Holocaust

[24] Winston Churchill

[25] The Japanese attacked Pearl Harbor.

[26] Franklin D. Roosevelt

[27] the Allies; the side with Great Britain, France, and the United States

[28] Mohandas Gandhi

[29] The United States and the Soviet Union

[30] the Cold War

[31] the Berlin Wall

[32] John Paul II

[33] Ronald Reagan

Activity 2: End of Semester *(Online)*

ASSESS

Semester Assessment: History 4, Semester 2 (*Offline*)

Complete an offline Semester Assessment. Your learning coach will score this part of the assessment.

Name _____   Date _____

Final Review and Assessment

Match the item on the left with the reason it is important on the right. Write the correct letter on the blank line.

1. _D_ Pearl Harbor
   communist
   lands

   _C_ Kitty Hawk, North Carolina
   battles

   _B_ Flanders Fields
   successful

   _E_ Hiroshima
   the

   _A_ Iron Curtain
   bomb

A. imaginary barrier between
   and democratic

B. site of famous World War I

C. location of the f rst
   airplane f ight

D. U.S. naval base attacked by
   Japanese

E. city where the f rst atomic
   was dropped

Read each question and its answer choices. Fill in the bubble in front of the best answer.

2. What does the "Age of Imperialism" refer to?

   ⓐ A time when democratic nations became industrial

   ⓑ A period when Gandhi and Mao fought for larger Asian empires

   ⓒ A time when industrial nations established colonies overseas

   ⓓ A period of invention and innovation in medicine and industry

3. This British writer lived in India, wrote children's stories, and was proud of the British empire. Who was he?

(a) Rudyard Kipling

(b) Winston Churchill

(c) David Livingstone

(d) Alexander Graham Bell

4. The lightbulb and phonograph have been invented. Mr. Bell has placed a telephone call. Mr. Andrew Carnegie is now making a fortune in steel. What year is it?

(a) 1800

(b) 1900

(c) 1950

(d) 1776

5. The assembly line I developed made it much easier and much cheaper to produce cars. Who am I?

(a) Henry Ford

(b) Karl Daimler

(c) Andrew Carnegie

(d) Louis Pasteur

6. Which of the following describes Thomas Edison?

   (a)   Chief engineer of the Panama Canal

   (b)   Ingenious inventor, known as "the Wizard of Menlo Park"

   (c)   Designer of the f rst airplane, regarded as "the f rst in f ight"

   (d)   Chemist who f gured out how to kill harmful bacteria

7. Which bodies of water does the Panama Canal connect?

   (a)   Mediterranean and Red Seas

   (b)   Yellow and Yangtze Rivers

   (c)   Atlantic Ocean and Great Lakes

   (d)   Atlantic and Pacif c Oceans

8. Which war was called "the Great War" or "the war to make the world safe for democracy"?

   (a)   World War II

   (b)   World War I

   (c)   The Spanish-American War

   (d)   The Cold War

9. What does women's suffrage refer to?

   ⓐ   The right of women to vote

   ⓑ   The ability of women to suffer silently

   ⓒ   The vaccination of women against polio

   ⓓ   The right of women to protest

10. How can we describe the peace that followed World War I?

   ⓐ   A time of prosperity and international cooperation

   ⓑ   A time of resentment, depression, and unrest

   ⓒ   A time of new democratic gains in Germany and Italy

   ⓓ   A time of nuclear threat and east-west tension

11. Who were Hitler, Mussolini, and Stalin?

   ⓐ   Communists who began the Cold War

   ⓑ   Founders of the United Nations

   ⓒ   Dictators who came to power in the 1930s

   ⓓ   Leaders in the war against tyranny

12. What do Alexander Fleming and Jonas Salk have in common?

   (a) They were both pioneers in medicine.

   (b) They were both leaders of independence movements.

   (c) They were both inventors who modernized cities.

   (d) They were both helpful with the Marshall Plan.

13. What were the League of Nations and the United Nations?

   (a) Alliances formed in time of war

   (b) International organizations formed to promote peace

   (c) Anti-colonial movements against European powers

   (d) Medical organizations providing disaster relief

14. In her later life, Eleanor Roosevelt worked with the United Nations to

   (a) advocate space travel.

   (b) promote human rights.

   (c) get computers in schools.

   (d) end British rule in India.

15. Even though there was a lot of war and bloodshed in the twentieth century, there was also

    (a) great progress in communication, transportation, and medicine.

    (b) peace and good will for most people of eastern Europe.

    (c) growing awareness that communism brought prosperity to its citizens.

    (d) an important treaty that eliminated all nuclear weapons.

16. He led the United States through the Great Depression and most of World War II. Who was he?

    (a) Harry Truman

    (b) John F. Kennedy

    (c) Ronald Reagan

    (d) Franklin Roosevelt

17. In 1957 the Soviet Union sent *Sputnik*, the f rst man-made satellite, into space. President John F. Kennedy responded by urging the United States to

    (a) send a missile to shoot down the Soviet satellite

    (b) land a man on the moon before the end of the 1960s

    (c) cooperate with the Soviet Union in developing new spacecraft

    (d) send troops to attack the Soviet Union

18. One of the greatest horrors of World War II was Hitler's attempt to kill all the Jews in Europe. What was that attempt called?

    ⓐ   D-Day

    ⓑ   *Blitzkrieg*

    ⓒ   The Cold War

    ⓓ   The Holocaust

19. What was Mohandas Gandhi's Salt March?

    ⓐ   Part of a campaign to free India from British Rule

    ⓑ   A military march from Calcutta to Delhi

    ⓒ   Part of a campaign to institute communism in India

    ⓓ   An attempt to supply India with salt from the ocean

20. Which American president said, "Mr. Gorbachev, tear down this wall"?

    ⓐ   Franklin Roosevelt

    ⓑ   Harry Truman

    ⓒ   John F. Kennedy

    ⓓ   Ronald Reagan

21. At the end of World War II, what did the victors do?

   (a)   They forced Germany, Italy, and Japan to pay reparations for their evil deeds.

   (b)   They turned Africa and Asia into colonial empires under Allied rule.

   (c)   They divided up the land of the Axis powers and kept it for themselves.

   (d)   They helped rebuild the economies and governments of war-torn nations.

22. What do we call the time when Czar Nicholas was ousted and Lenin came to power?

   (a)   The Russian Revolution

   (b)   The Cultural Revolution

   (c)   The Cold War

   (d)   The Soviet Supremacy

23. Who led the British during the Battle of Britain and proved to be one of the greatest leaders England ever had?

   (a)   David Livingstone

   (b)   Winston Churchhill

   (c)   Queen Victoria

   (d)   Dwight Eisenhower

24. How did Charles Lindbergh lift people's spirits in the 1920s?

(a)   He invented the f rst antibiotic.

(b)   He f ew solo between New York and Paris.

(c)   He became a champion f agpole sitter.

(d)   He discovered a way to make computers small.

25. What have the governments of Lenin, Stalin, and Mao shown about communism?

(a)   It tends to make people free and increase their standard of living.

(b)   It encourages religious worship and promotes great art.

(c)   It puts power in the hands of few, and takes freedom away from many.

(d)   It does not encourage advances in science or technology.

26. The Cold War ended when the Berlin Wall fell and the Soviet Union broke apart. Why were people so happy the Cold War ended?

(a)   There was less threat of another world war.

(b)   There was a greater chance for freedom and democracy in Eastern Europe and elsewhere.

(c)   The deadly threat of communism was over.

(d)   All of the above